ON

SCHOPENHAUER

S. Jack Odell
University of Maryland

WADSWORTH

THOMSON LEARNING

Australia • Canada • Mexico • Singapore • Spain
United Kingdom • United States

This book is dedicated to my best friend, Boo Bradford.

*I want to thank my wife, Barbara Reed Bradford,
for her diligent editing of this book, and I want to thank
the series editor, Dr. Daniel Kolak, for his encouragement.*

Printed in the United States of America
1 2 3 4 5 6 7 04 03 02 01 00

For permission to use material from this text, contact us:
Web: http://www.thomsonrights.com
Fax: 1-800-730-2215
Phone: 1-800-730-2214

For more information, contact:
Wadsworth/Thomson Learning, Inc.
10 Davis Drive
Belmont, CA 94002-3098
USA
http://www.wadsworth.com

ISBN: 0-534-57633-8

Contents

Introduction

Few philosophers are more fascinating than Schopenhauer. A first encounter with Schopenhauer is an unforgettable experience. Most philosophers and most people are appalled either by the man, his philosophy, or both. By temperament he was irascible, volatile, egoistic, pessimistic, even cruel. But in spite of his temperament, he was quite charming and enormously entertaining when he wanted to be. He was famously witty. His philosophy of life was deeply pessimistic. Nevertheless, or perhaps because of his pessimism, he is one of the most intriguing and interesting philosophers who ever put a quill to parchment, or, for that matter, any writing instrument to any kind of surface or material. He shocks and surprises us. He annoys and amuses us. His views about most subjects are profound and penetrating even if somewhat off-putting. He attacks every view we treasure. He tantalizes and then disappoints us. Most people are repelled by his pessimism. He maintained that the natural condition for humanity was pain and suffering, that happiness and contentment were momentary and transitive phenomena. Nonetheless, he has had a powerful influence upon the history of thought. He influenced Nietzsche, Freud, Wagner, D. H. Lawrence, Thomas Mann, Joseph Conrad, Leo Tolstoy, Marcel Proust, and the twentieth century's most important philosopher, Ludwig Wittgenstein.

In spite of the originality of Schopenhauer's philosophy and the many notable figures it has influenced, it has not received much attention in the twentieth century. Bertrand Russell, in his influential and widely read *History of Western Philosophy*, expresses what I think

1

has been the view of many twentieth century philosophers concerning Schopenhauer's philosophy. He considers Schopenhauer to have only importance as a "stage in historical development." His pessimism is viewed by Russell to have served as the antithesis to the optimism advocated and defended by most philosophers, and is "useful in bringing forward considerations which would otherwise" have been "overlooked." Not that either pessimism or optimism is, for Russell, acceptable. Belief in either position "is a matter of temperament, and not of reason," according to Russell. Russell does begrudgingly acknowledge that Schopenhauer's doctrine of the primacy of the will has influenced many, including Nietzsche, Bergson, James, and Dewey, and for that reason, it too is, "in spite of inconsistency and a certain shallowness," of importance as a "stage in historical development," but not of lasting value. Because, as he also says, "in proportion as will has gone up in the scale, knowledge has gone down."[1]

Happily, renewed interest in his work has increased in the last twenty years—although it should be mentioned that Michael Gardner published an excellent book on Schopenhauer in 1963.[2] In 1980, Michael Fox, in his "Preface" to *Schopenhauer: His Philosophical Achievement*, a collection of essays on Schopenhauer which he edited, described his subject as "one of the nineteenth-century's most original and penetrating thinkers."[3] He also expressed the hope that "the present anthology, with the many perspectives it contains, can contribute to a more realistic assessment of Schopenhauer's significance."[4] Whether because of this anthology, which I praised in a review for *Teaching Philosophy*,[5] or because of it and other works that appeared around the same time, there has been a bit of a renaissance regarding Schopenhauer's work. Another book on Schopenhauer, which I also favorably reviewed for *Teaching Philosophy*,[6] is D. W. Hamlyn's *Schopenhauer*. Hamlyn, like Fox, expresses an overall positive view of Schopenhauer. One of the most compelling and interesting books on Schopenhauer to appear during this Schopenhauer renaissance is Bryan Magee's *The Philosophy of Schopenhauer*. Magee is a devoted fan of Schopenhauer, and his enthusiasm is communicable. In a review I wrote about it, I described it as "informative, provocative, original, and well written."[7]

Schopenhauer has the ability to undermine our basic beliefs while at the same time forcing us to consider altogether unsatisfactory replacements. Nietzsche, who was much influenced by Schopenhauer, also has that ability. Hegel, whom Schopenhauer both hated and envied, is also exciting and surprising, but his style is extremely off-putting. His ponderous, tortured, and convoluted style is enough to convince most readers that German writers are dedicated sadists in search of a masochistic audience. Both Nietzsche and Schopenhauer are exceptions to this unhappy practice. They are enjoyable to read both in German and in translation. Of the two, Schopenhauer is the more readable in so far as his meaning is always transparently present. Excesses in poetic license rarely ever obscure it. Nietzsche's desire to impress the reader with his artistic ability tends sometimes to obscure his conceptual intentions.

No other philosopher had a greater influence upon Schopenhauer than did Kant. Schopenhauer was both influenced and inspired by Kant's philosophy. He referred to Kant in *The Fourfold Root of the Principle of Sufficient Reason* as the "marvelous Kant." Kant's philosophy, which he would eventually criticize, served him as a springboard, off of which he dived headlong into the dark and murky seas of the transcendental. Schopenhauer's basic ideas were borrowed from Kant. Kant's distinction between the *noumenal* and the *phenomenal* was incorporated into Schopenhauer's metaphysics. According to Kant, there is the world as we perceive and know, and there is the world as it is in itself—independent of our various perceptions of it. Kant claimed that we could not know this latter world—the noumenal world. For Kant, this is a logical or conceptual necessity. To know is to perceive. Since the noumenal is the world unperceived, it cannot be known. It can only be perceived.

Schopenhauer appreciated Kant's logic, but considered him to be mistaken as regards the possibility of knowing the noumenal. He regarded the noumenal to be directly, if not completely, known. He considered it to be animal will or striving. It is this point of disagreement with Kant that is, in essence, Schopenhauer's philosophy.

Next to Kant, Plato was the most fruitful sources for ideas upon which Schopenhauer relied to carve out his image of the meaning and end of human existence. Schopenhauer was a self-acknowledged student of Plato. He was also a student of the Buddha, and of classical Hinduism.

Plato, who Schopenhauer described in both his *Fourfold Root of the Principle of Sufficient Reason*, and *The World as Will and Representation* as "divine," like Kant, distinguished between the transitory world of appearances on the one hand, and the real world on the other. The everyday world, knowledge of which is primarily provided by sense experience, is, for Plato, the *world of appearance*—in his cave metaphor, it is the shadows of reality cast upon the wall by the illumination of the sun, a metaphor for the form of the "Good." The real world, the *Logos*, consists of underlying forms or "ideas." The Logos corresponds to Kant's noumenal world, and the world of appearance to Kant's phenomenal world. There is an important difference between these two philosophers, however, and it concerns the possibility of knowledge of the underlying reality. Kant, as I previously noted, proclaimed skepticism regarding its nature. One knows that it exists. Its existence can be demonstrated. But its nature is of necessity a mystery. For Plato, we can and do know reality. We do, on occasion, directly know it. We do so as disembodied spirits. Plato believed in transmigration of souls. Each of us is in reality a disembodied spirit, but we are forced to spend much of eternity as embodied creatures of appearance. We die and are reborn in an endless cycle of being. Every time one of us dies, we are transported to the Logos—which serves as a transfer point at which we wait for our next body. This transfer point is not without its reward, however. Here we "see," are put in direct contact with the eternal forms, including that most supreme forms—the form of the "Good." This way station becomes in, Christianity, a metaphor for heaven or the after life, and the form of the "Good" is transformed into the face of God.

Classical Hinduism likewise insists upon the distinction between the empirical or everyday world and its underlying reality. The every day world, *Maya*, is illusion. *Brahma* is the real world. Like Plato, classical Hinduism allows for knowledge of the real world. It also promulgates the idea of transmigration. On the subject of transmigration it does, however, differ from Plato's account. When one knows or become one with the underlying reality one achieves *Nirvana*. One has to become "ready" for it. But one has little control over this readiness. One passes from one form of being to another until one is fortunate enough to become one of those beings that can achieve *Nirvana*. Such individuals are recognizable, however. They are the holy men or mystics one encounters from time to time, particularly in India.

Buddha, brought up on Hinduism, departed from it and taught his followers a different kind of creed. He claimed that anyone who realizes certain truths, and follows a specifiable course of action, could, in his lifetime, succeed in attaining *nirvana*. The truths that one must accept are referred to as "The Four Noble Truths." They are: (1) that

4

life is filled with suffering; (2) that its cause is wrongly directed desire
or will; (3) that if we remove the wrong desire, suffering will be abated;
and (4) that the way to dispense with wrong desire is the "Noble
Eightfold Path." The "Noble Eightfold Path," or course of action
necessary for the attainment of "enlightenment," consists in
developing: (a) right understanding; (b) right thinking; (c) right speech
habits; (d) right behavior; (e) right employment; (f) right effort; (g)
right concentration; and (h) right meditation. Schopenhauer agreed
with the Buddha regarding the unhappiness that will or striving created.
And he looked to asceticism as the best means for attaining happiness,
but disagreed that it was ultimately attainable.

Hegel, on the other hand, did not influence Schopenhauer. In fact,
he was hated by Schopenhauer. Schopenhauer regarded him as a
pretentious windbag and charlatan. No doubt, his hatred of Hegel was
fueled by jealousy. Hegel was immensely popular, and Schopenhauer
was not. And when their paths crossed, Schopenhauer was always the
loser.[8]

Ludwig Wittgenstein, on the other hand, was much influenced by
Schopenhauer. Elizabeth Anscombe has recounted Wittgenstein's
having acknowledged that he had read Schopenhauer during his
teenage years, and that he had at that time been convinced that
Schopenhauer's philosophy was essentially right, that only minor
adjustments were needed to ratify its faults.[9] He is also reputed to have
kept only two books by his bedside, one of which was, *The World as
Will and Representation.*

Also, Schopenhauer had a profound influence upon the writer
Thomas Mann. Mann claims that Schopenhauer's philosophy was not
simply relevant for his time, but relevant to the future development of
our species. His philosophy, according to Mann, may yet help "bring
to birth a new humanity of which we stand in need." It is in fact, my
opinion that it is Mann who, of all commentators on Schopenhauer's
philosophy, offers one of the best summaries of it. He says:

> Indeed, all the textbooks tell us that Schopenhauer is first the
> philosopher of the will and second the philosopher of pessimism.
> But actually there is no first and second, for they are one and the
> same, and he was the second by virtue of his being the first; he
> was necessarily pessimist because he was the philosopher and
> psychologist of the will. Will, as the opposite pole of inactive
> satisfaction, is naturally a fundamental unhappiness, it is unrest, a

striving for *something*—it is want, craving, avidity, demand, suffering; and a world of will can be nothing else but a world of suffering.[10]

Schopenhauer's influence over Tolstoy was intense and lasted for many years. Schopenhauer's work so impressed Tolstoy that he encouraged others to translate Schopenhauer into Russian so that those, unlike himself, who could not read German, would have access to this philosophy. In "My Confession," he acknowledged Schopenhauer's influence, which he equated to that of the Brahmins and Solomon, as a necessary step along the way towards his own eventual commitment to the idea that *faith* alone provides the solution to the meaning of life question. It was not the fact that he "along with Solomon and Schopenhauer, did not kill" themselves that convinced him that life was worth living. Instead, it was "the existence of faith," in the hearts of those millions of Christians that provided, in opposition to Schopenhauer et al, the meaning of life.[11]

According to Bryan Magee, the thoughts of the great German composer Wagner concerning life and the cosmos were greatly changed as a direct result of his having discovered *The World as Will and Representation*, and this change in outlook had consequences on Wagner's music. Magee claims that Wagner's creative work "from this time on takes a new direction and that everything subsequently produced would have had a very different form if Schopenhauer's influence had been absent."[12]

In this work, I will emphasize Schopenhauer's efforts to rectify Kant's philosophy by explicating the noumenal as the will to live, and I will critically explicate Plato's influence upon his views concerning art. I will critically examine Schopenhauer's views concerning the meaning and significance of human existence. They are among the most interesting aspects of his philosophy. In Chapter I, I will discuss Schopenhauer's life and character. In Chapter II, I will provide a historical setting for Schopenhauer's philosophy. My explication of Schopenhauer's philosophy will begin in Chapter III, which will be devoted to understanding his doctoral dissertation, *The Four fold Root of the Principle of Sufficient Reason*. Chapters IV, V, and VI will be devoted to his major accomplishment, *The World as Will and Representation*. My reason for proceeding in this way is that Schopenhauer's philosophy is best understood as a combination of both, *The Four fold Root of the Principle of Sufficient Reason* and *The World as Will and Representation*. They are two interlaced parts of the one philosophy that is Schopenhauer's. Chapter IV will be devoted to the first two sections of *The World as Will and Representation*. The first section contains his development of the thesis that the object and the subject are one—that the world is representation. The second section concerns his thesis that the thing-in-itself, Kant's noumenal world, is ultimately will. In Chapter V, I will discuss section three of *The World as Will and Representation*, which contains Schopenhauer's understanding of Plato's Forms and their role in his aesthetics. In Chapter VI, I will examine section four of Schopenhauer's major work, which involves his views on morality, the philosophy of life, and the importance of asceticism.

---

[1] Russell (1945) pp. 758-759.
[2] Gardner (1963). This book influenced both Hamlyn and Magee.
[3] Fox (1980) p. xv.
[4] Ibid., p. xvii.
[5] Odell (1983-A).
[6] Odell (1983-B).
[7] Odell (1985).
[8] See below, p. 10.
[9] Anscombe (1959) p. 11.
[10] Mann (1939) reprinted in Fox (1980) p. 7.
[11] Tolstoy (1905) reprinted in Klemke (1981) pp. 16-17.
[12] Magee (1983) p. 349.

I
Schopenhauer's Life and Character

Schopenhauer was neither a happy nor a contented man. He was not a praiseworthy one either. While passing judgment upon Schopenhauer's doctrine that "one may diminish the quantity of evil by weakening the will," which is accomplished by practicing "complete chastity, voluntary poverty, fasting, and self-torture," Bertrand Russell paints the following picture of his subject's character:

> Nor is the doctrine sincere, if we may judge by Schopenhauer's life. He habitually dined well, at a good restaurant; he had many trivial love affairs, which were sensual but not passionate; he was exceedingly quarrelsome and unusually avaricious. On one occasion he was annoyed by an elderly seamstress who was talking to a friend outside the door of his apartment. He threw her downstairs causing her permanent injury. She obtained a court order compelling him to pay her a certain sum (15 thalers) every quarter for as long as she lived. When at last she died, after twenty years, he noted in his account book: "Obit anus, abit onus," [which Russell translates as "The old woman dies, the burden departs."] It is hard to find in his life evidences of any

virtue except kindness to animals, which he carried to the point of objecting to vivisection in the interests of science. In all other respects he was completely selfish. It is difficult to believe that a man who was profoundly convinced of the virtue of asceticism and resignation would never have made any attempt to embody his convictions in his practice.[1]

In defense of Schopenhauer, lest one be carried away by Russell's fallacious (*ad hominum*) attack on the man and his philosophy, the incident concerning the "seamstress" can be sorted out differently and more sympathetically for Schopenhauer. Bryan Magee does so in his book on Schopenhauer, where he describes the victim of Schopenhauer's assault as a housekeeper. According to Magee, this woman and other housekeepers frequently congregated outside Schopenhauer's door, when he working, and engaged in loud conversation. Schopenhauer complained about it but they persisted. And one day when three of them were congregated outside his door, he asked them to leave. Two did, but one refused. He persisted in his demand that she leave, but she stubbornly declined his invitation. They got into a shoving match, and he shoved her down the stairs causing her serious injury. In his defense Magee observes, "No doubt this [the loud conversations of the housekeepers] was a genuine nuisance to someone doing his kind of work, but over and above that he had a nervous aversion to noise and was apt to lose control of his temper when subjected to it."[2]

Magee's version of the incident in question mitigates somewhat Russell's indictment of Schopenhauer. But his version of what happened years later when the housekeeper died is even more chilling than Russell's version. According to Magee, when she died, Schopenhauer was sent a copy of her death certificate, and it was upon it that he wrote "Obit anus, abit onus." In neither version is the issue of whether he threw her down the steps or she fell down them herself as a result of their skirmish resolved. If the former is what actually happened, Schopenhauer's guilt is much greater than if the latter is what happened. Moreover, we need to know whether it was the housekeeper who attacked him, and he defended himself, or if it was Schopenhauer who initiated the action, and she was just defending herself when he shoved her or she fell as a result of their shoving match. We will probably never know what actually transpired. But in any case his actions cannot be completely vindicated. He did engage in "physical combat" with a woman, and as a result she was badly

9

harmed, and what is more damaging than this to his character is his emotional indifference to her death.

Very few of his contemporaries were at all fond of him. He was inconsiderate, self-centered, spiteful, and jealous of the success of others. It was professional jealousy that motivated him to schedule his lectures, during his brief academic career, at the same hour as those of Hegel. Hegel was at the time immensely popular, both among students and intellectuals. Schopenhauer hoped to gain a large following and embarrass Hegel. Instead, no one came to his lectures, and Hegel's lectures were filled—standing room only. This was to be the end of Schopenhauer's academic career. He never again donned the robes and placed upon his head a mortarboard. This all happened at the University of Berlin in 1920, just prior to his scuffle with the housekeeper. He was still recoiling from his humiliation nearly thirty years later, when, in the "Author's Preface" to the 1847 edition of *The Fourfold Root of the Principle of Sufficient Reason* (originally published in 1813), he viciously described Hegel as a "charlatan." Unable to let the matter rest with this stain on Hegel's character he adds:

> The minds of the present generation of scholars are disorganized by Hegelian nonsense; incapable of thinking, course and stupefied, they become the prey to the shallow materialism that has crept out of the basilisk's egg.

Schopenhauer was born in Danzig (now Gdansk) on February 22, 1788. He was the son of a wealthy businessman and a cultivated and enthusiastic mother who had serious intellectual interests. His father's family was quite prominent. Peter the Great and the Empress Catherine had stayed with Schopenhauer's grandfather when they visited Danzig in 1716. Frederick the Great personally tried to induce Schopenhauer's father to move from Danzig to Prussia. His parents were both worldly and sophisticated. They were world travelers and young Arthur greatly benefited from this aspect of their lifestyle. He was able to learn a great deal about the world at an early age because he was exposed to so much of it. During his youth he spent enough time in both Paris and London to become fluent in both French and English. His English was exemplary.

Schopenhauer's father tried to arrange things in such a way as to guarantee that his son would be an English citizen. He planned to take his wife to England for Schopenhauer's birth, but providence interfered, she became ill, and Schopenhauer became a native son of Danzig. In 1793, the Prussians captured Danzig, and the family moved to Hamburg where they resided until Schopenhauer's father died in 1805. During this period, the family traveled extensively, particularly between 1803 and 1805, when they spent the whole two years touring Europe. At one point, when Schopenhauer was only nine years old, he was left in Le Havre with a business associate for a period of two years. It was during this time that Schopenhauer became proficient in French. When Schopenhauer was seventeen, his father's drowned body was discovered in a canal near his business warehouse. Although his death was ruled to be accidental, he was suspected of having committed suicide. He had for some time previous to his death been deeply depressed.

After his father's death, Schopenhauer's mother Johanna left him in Hamburg in charge of the family business and moved to Weimar. There she established herself as what can only be described, to borrow from the Hollywood vernacular, the "hostess with the mostest." Her salon was attended by many of the most famous literati, artists and musicians of the time. Goethe, Schubert, and the Grimm brothers were often in attendance there. She began to write herself. She wrote romance novels that were very popular. During this time, when his mother was flourishing in Weimar, Schopenhauer became more and more disenchanted with the life of a businessman, and pleaded with his mother to allow him to pursue the intellectual life. She agreed, and he left Hamburg, to enroll in the Gymnasium in Gotha.

At Gotha, Schopenhauer studied Greek, Latin, History, and Mathematics. At the age of twenty-one, in 1809, he entered the University of Göttingen. There he studied physics, natural history, astronomy, meteorology, physiology, botany, law, and eventually philosophy. He attended lectures on Plato and Kant. He was both a marvelously gifted and assiduously persistent student. In 1811, he transferred to the University of Berlin, where he studied under Fichte and Schleiermacher. He was not, however, much impressed with either philosopher, though he did not develop the same intense hatred of Schleiermacher that he did of Fichte. He thought Fichte was a pretentious phony. He viewed Fichte as one who was only in philosophy for egoistic reasons.

Schopenhauer left the University of Berlin after only two years, and took up residence in the country, and it was there that he wrote his doctoral dissertation, *The Fourfold Root of the Principle of Sufficient Reason*. It took him only a year to complete it. When it was finished,

11

he submitted it to the University of Jena rather than the University of Berlin, possibly, because he was so dissatisfied with the philosophy faculty at Berlin. Jena granted him a doctorate in philosophy.

Around the time he received his doctorate, he moved in with his mother. They quarreled. He moved out and never saw her again. She died in 1838. She was self-centered, and apparently cared very little for motherhood. After her husband's death, she did her best to avoid having Schopenhauer around. Schopenhauer never got along with anyone for very long, perhaps, in part at any rate, because of his relationship with his mother. Brian Magee blames her for Schopenhauer's pessimism. He claims that "there can be little doubt that Schopenhauer's despairing view of the world, above all his conviction of the terribleness of existence *as such*, were in some degree neurotic manifestations which had their roots in his relationship with his mother."[3] Perhaps Magee is correct, but I do not think one should rule out genetics. His father was prone to brooding and unhappiness, and as I pointed out previously, may well have been so disturbed that he took his own life.

During the years between 1814 and 1818, Schopenhauer took up residence in Dresden, and it was there that he wrote the first edition of his major work, *The World as Will and Representation*. After completing this work, he journeyed to Italy, spending considerable time in Venice. He thoroughly enjoyed himself during this period. He is reputed to have on one occasion, while out walking with his current love interest, encountered Lord Byron, who was at that time also residing in Venice. One cannot resist speculating about what must have transpired between these two tempestuous lovers of the good things in life. Perhaps they dined together, sharing stories of their many conquests, while comparing notes on the quality of the wine and cuisine available to them. They probably tried hard to out do one another. Neither was remotely modest, and both possessed immense egos.

Eventually Schopenhauer tired of the good life, and returned to Germany, where he made an attempt to become a professional academic. He took up residence in Berlin, but meet with little success at the University there. It was during this stay in Berlin that he developed his hatred for Hegel. He came to hate Hegel even more than he hated Fichte—a fact probably best explained by events I referred to earlier in this chapter concerning Schopenhauer's having scheduled his lectures at the same time as Hegel. It must have been largely due to the fact that the students totally absented themselves from his lectures that

Schopenhauer gave up all hopes for an academic life.

He left Berlin after this disappointment and, as was his habit throughout the first half of his life, he spent time traveling about Europe. In 1831, he moved to Frankfort, where he lived for only about a year before moving to Mannheim. He moved to Mannheim on orders from his doctor, who thought that a change of scenery would help him recover from an extended bout of depression. In 1833, he moved back to Frankfort where he continued to live until his death in 1860. He was seventy-two when he died. Given the reported symptoms his death was probably due to a heart attack, but because of the state of medicine at the time, it could have been caused by any number of other ailments.

By all accounts, Schopenhauer was in his youth a good-looking fellow, well dressed and witty, and with an eye for the opposite sex. Throughout his life he remained sexually active, though he never married. In the evening of his life, he finally received the attention he had sought all his life. His major work, *The World as Will and Representation*, was virtually ignored for years. It was not until the late 1840's that it received any attention. At this time, while living out his remaining years in a hotel, his reputation began to spread, and he spent his last few years basking in his newly acquired fame. He died a happy pessimist!

---

[1] Russell (1945) p. 758.
[2] Magee (1983) fn., p. 12.
[3] Ibid., p. 13.

I
Historical Setting

Our understanding of Schopenhauer's philosophy will be made easier if we place it in the wider context of modern philosophy i.e., philosophy after 1500, and will be made much easier if we place it in the context of Kant's philosophy. In fact, it is hard to imagine how one could come to fully appreciate what Schopenhauer was attempting to accomplish without an understanding of certain elements of Kantian philosophy. In this chapter, I will first of all hit the high spots of modern philosophy which to some extent dictated the course that Kant's philosophy would travel, and I will explain those aspects of Kant's philosophy which motivated Schopenhauer. He saw himself as a modifier of Kant's philosophy.

Modern philosophy inherited from ancient and medieval philosophy what can best be described as *substance philosophy*—that is, that the universe consists of basic, and irreducible substance or substances. Descartes, the first great modern philosopher, declared that there were, with the exception of God, two and only two basic substances: mind or mental substance; and matter or physical substance. Mind is the subject of knowledge, and matter its object. Mind is inherently a knowing subject for Descartes, and it *innately* knows most of what is most important to know. For Descartes, the mental substance has an understanding of God as perfection. Through our minds, mental substances, we innately know a variety of principles, for example, the causality principle that every event has a cause, and the so called "laws of thought:" the principle of contradiction, which

14

says no proposition is both true and false at one and the same time; the principle of identity, which says that a thing is identical with itself; and the law of excluded middle, which says that every proposition is either true or false. Descartes and his followers, which included Leibniz and Spinoza, came to be known as *rationalists*. Rationalism flourished upon the continent of Europe. It did not fare so well on the British Isles. It came under attack in England by a group of philosophers led by John Locke, and this group of philosophers came to be known as the *empiricists*.

Locke retained both mental substance and material substance, but argued that the mind is at birth a *blank tablet*, upon which its scribe, sensory experience, writes the whole of what can be there recorded. For Locke, there can be *no* innate knowledge. All knowledge is perceptual knowledge. According to Locke, external objects (material substances) tables, chairs, etc. produce (cause) in our minds (mental substances) "ideas" of themselves and their qualities. This view of his is known as *the causal theory of perception*. There are, according to Locke, two kinds of qualities of physical objects—primary qualities, and secondary ones. The primary qualities are said to be inherent in the objects (tables, chairs, etc.) themselves. The secondary qualities exist only in our minds. The objects in themselves consist of primary qualities: size, shape, solidity, motion, and number. The secondary qualities are: colors, sounds, tastes, and smells, and they only exist in our minds, but they are caused to exist there by powers inherent in the primary qualities of the objects themselves. If an apple is divided into parts however small, its parts will all have a shape, a size, solidity, be in motion or in rest, and be denumerable. If, however, an apple is divided into smaller and smaller parts, it will eventually lose its color, smell, taste, and will make no sounds. So, while our ideas of primary color are of things inherent in their causes, our ideas of secondary qualities exist only in our minds. This doctrine created insoluble problems, problems voiced by Locke's most influential followers, Berkeley and Hume.

The principle problem this view creates is that if the mind is *only* aware of its ideas, how can it ever know that they correspond to the qualities that are actually possessed by the underlying material things-in-themselves? It has no way of comparing its ideas with the things-in-themselves. Berkeley tried to escape from this dilemma by doing away with material substance altogether, and espousing metaphysical idealism. He claimed that there is only mental substance and its ideas. Material substance is a myth. Knowledge, for Berkeley, is restricted to knowledge of the mental substance and its ideas. Instead of inferring the existence of the causes (material substances) on the basis of the existence of our ideas of these causes, Berkeley claimed that tables, chairs, etc. are just bundles of ideas, and that, for example, the claim "That is a table," means only that I am at present experiencing ideas of a given sort, and if I were to engage in actions of a specific sort, I would have further experiences of a specifiable sort. The causal inference is now from present ideas to future ideas. The theory of perception Berkeley espoused is known as *phenomenalism*.

Hume, on the other hand, claimed that it is impossible to resolve the discrepancy that obtains between the sensory data and the independent existence of its alleged causes. The existence of the sensory givens is indisputable, but its indisputable claim for its own existence cannot, as a matter of logic, says Hume, be carried over and attached to things defined as existing independent of them. Moreover, unlike the rationalists, Hume reduces the causality principle, that every event has a cause, to a mere empirical generalization based solely upon temporal association, B's always following A. We may think that the concept of causation is somehow based upon the existence of a necessary connection between the cause and effect, but this is an illusion.

What follows from these considerations is that the empiricist must redefine material objects and adopt some form of phenomenalism, or affirm *skepticism* and deny both that one has knowledge of independently existing chairs, tables, etc., or that anyone can ever know that any B will result from any A. Neither of these options necessitated by empiricism is a happy one. Nor, for that matter is the innatism of rationalism, especially when viewed from the perspective that Hume brought to bear upon such alleged innate ideas as the causal principle. This is, at any rate, how Kant perceived the situation in philosophy when he arrived upon the scene.

Kant credited Hume with "awakening him" from the dogmatic slumbers induced in him by his teachers, teachers who were inclined towards rationalism, which was homegrown on the continent. Hume convinced him that the principle of causality could not be justified on empirical grounds, but he was not willing to stomach Hume's explanation that the idea of its necessity was illusory. For Kant, the idea that every event has a cause is an *apriori* truth not simply an illusion based upon the mere association of ideas. Here he sides with the rationalists, but he is unwilling to accept their explanation of how such knowledge is possible. The idea that every event has a cause is

16

for the rationalist a full blown innately known truth. For Kant, the explanation of its truth is more complex. Kant's explanation of the possibility of *apriori* knowledge begins with the distinction between analytic and *synthetic* judgments. The former are said by Kant to be those judgments the predicate of which is contained, at the least implicitly, in the subject. He regards the latter to be those judgments the predicates of which are *not* contained in the subjects. An example of the former would be the judgment that all triangles are three-sided figures. The predicate "is a three-sided figure" is contained in the subject "triangle." An independent test for a proposition or claim being analytic is whether or not its denial infringes the principle of contradiction, one of the three laws of thought I mentioned previously. If the denial of a claim or proposition is a contradiction, then that claim or proposition is analytic. Since a triangle is by definition a three-sided figure, the claim that a triangle is not a three-sided figure is a contradiction since it both affirms and denies that a triangle is three-sided.

An example of a synthetic judgment would be that my dog is brown. The idea of "brownness" is not contained in, or part of, the definition of the word 'dog.' It is only through experience that we learn that some dogs are brown. For this reason, synthetic judgments are said by Kant to be true *a posteriori*, in contrast to analytic judgments, which are said to be known to be true *a priori*—independent of experience. On the basis of this, one might conclude that all analytic judgments are *a priori* and all synthetic ones are *a posteriori*. This is, in essence, just what Hume concluded, and it remained true for those twentieth century empiricists—the logical positivists. The implication of this view of the matter is, as Kant understood it, and as it was understood and promulgated by the positivists, that metaphysics, understood as the science of being, is impossible. Metaphysics does not concern itself with analytic propositions, propositions the denials of which are contradictory. Such propositions say nothing about reality. But metaphysics does not concern itself with *a posteriori* synthetic propositions either. They constitute the proper domain of empirical science. If metaphysics were conceived of as fundamentally concerned with *a posteriori* propositions, philosophy would have to be considered to be just another empirical science. This was inconceivable to Kant, but many contemporary philosophers do not view it that way. It is, in fact, the creed of the cognitive scientists that sound philosophy is inseparable from science.

17

For Kant, however, and this is of the essence of his philosophy, some synthetic, judgments are *a priori*. Judgments in mathematics, for example "seven plus five equals twelve," are synthetic *a priori*. According to Kant, the concept of "twelve" does not contain within itself the concepts of "seven" and "five," and is therefore not analytic, but is instead synthetic, yet universally true, and so it has to be *a priori*.[1] For Kant, these synthetic *a priori* judgments are the domain of the metaphysician.

Metaphysics attempts to say what is true of reality, but non verifiable in experience. Kant argues that the causal principle is itself an example of a synthetic *a priori* judgment. His reason for this conclusion is that the predicate, "being caused," is not contained in the idea of "being an event." Yet the principle is understood to apply universally and not just to events which have or are happening. It applies as well to events that have not as yet happened. Its truth then cannot be based upon what has happened. It establishes a *necessary connection*, and not an empirical one, between an object and its cause. But how, asks Kant, is it possible for the objects of knowledge to cause in us the concept of necessity when it is not an observable or empirical given? How can it be that the mind conforms to the objects of its knowledge; how, for example, can it be said to know regarding any object that it has been caused? Kant takes what he considers to be a Copernican step, and forces us to consider the conformity between object and subject to lie in the object's conforming to the subject. He says, "Failing of satisfactory progress in explaining the movements of the heavenly bodies on the supposition that they all revolve around the spectator, he [Copernicus] tried whether he might not have better success if he made the spectator to revolve and the stars to remain at rest."[2] He claims that his *Critique of Pure Reason* is founded upon the hypothesis that the objects of knowledge conform to the subject. To be an object of the understanding is, for Kant, to be subjected to the *a priori* nature of human understanding. The principle of causality is one of these givens. It is the subject who supplies the necessity inherent in our understanding that every object is caused to be. Kant insists that it is human understanding *conjoined* with human sensibility which defines the objects of possible knowledge. What we know as a table is not that thing in itself, as unperceived, but rather what it is as perceived, as a representation. The human intellect, of necessity, imposes upon the object-in-itself, in the very act of knowing it, its own natural or innate mechanisms. There is the table-in-itself, and there is the table-known. The table as it is known is understood to be, among other things it is understood to be, a spatio-temporal entity. Kant's doctrine that objects are, as known, nothing but representations of the things-in-themselves is *transcendental* idealism, as distinct from the idealism of Berkeley, which maintains that there are no material substances—that consciousness and its ideas are the only substances.

On Kant's account, it is the "categories of the sensibility and understanding" that are innate, and not, as the rationalists imagined, full-blown judgments. He agrees with the empiricists that it is through sensation that we know objects, but he wants it to be clearly understood that sensation involves a synthesis of form with matter, and thus the imposition of the forms of space and time. Objects cannot be sensed as they are in themselves, no more so than can an object seen through pink spectacles be seen as it is when seen without the use of pink spectacles. Sensation or "sense intuition" provides the intellect with an object already given in terms of form and matter, a material thing in space and time, subject to causation. Understanding then imposes its own mechanisms on these givens of sense experience. The inherent function of these mechanisms is to interpret the givens of sense, and thus the mechanisms of human understanding cannot be legitimately used with reference to entities that transcend experience. Philosophers who do so are engaged in a hopeless and illegitimate activity, which is, according to Kant, what was done by traditional metaphysicians.

For Kant, things-in-themselves, while conceivable, cannot be known. For Schopenhauer, this is where Kant fails. He claims that there is ultimately one and only one thing in-itself, and that we can and do know it. That one thing is, as we shall see, the will.

---

[1] Had it been possible for Kant to be made aware of Frege's distinction between the *sense* of an expression or sentence and the *reference* of an expression or sentence, he would probably have recognized that he was mistaken about the synthetic nature of mathematical judgments. What is referred to by the expression 'five,' would on Frege's account be, $1+1+1+1+1$ and by 'seven' would be $1+1+1+1+1+1+1$, which, when conjoined by an additional '+,' would be the same thing as what is referred to by 'twelve,' namely, $1+1+1+1+1 + 1+1+1+1+1+1+1$. To deny that five plus seven equals twelve would be seen on this account of the matter to contradict oneself, and thus the judgment that five plus seven equals twelve is really analytic, and not synthetic, *a priori*.

[2] Kant (1961) p. 22.

19

III

The Fourfold Root of
The Principle of Sufficient
Reason

Schopenhauer wrote *The Fourfold Root of the Principle of Sufficient Reason* in 1913 when he was twenty-five years old. It was his doctoral dissertation. It was, however, revised in 1847, and in the Preface of the 1847 edition he claimed:

> From the arrangement *now given* [the italics are mine] to some parts, we even have a compendious theory of the whole faculty of knowledge. But simply following the principle of sufficient reason, this theory presents the matter from a new and characteristic angle. But it is then supplemented by the first book of *The World as Will and Representation* together with the relevant chapters in the second volume of that work, and by the Criticism of the Kantian Philosophy to be found at the end of the first volume.[1]

In the light of these contentions, it would be unreasonable to conclude that the work in question was in its author's mind of lesser importance than his *The World as Will and Representation*. For Schopenhauer, the two works are just different parts of a single whole.

20

Interlaced, they provide a "compendious theory of the whole faculty of knowledge. In *The Fourfold Root*, Schopenhauer is sometimes interpreted to hold that, strictly speaking, there is not just one principle of sufficient reason but instead there are four, though they can be couched in an abbreviated form as "nothing is without a ground or reason why it is."[2] On this interpretation, the first of these *four principles of sufficient reason*, the first root, which has to do with *physical* change, can be stated as "nothing physical is without a cause." The *second principle of sufficient reason*, the second root, which has to do with *logical* derivation, can be stated as "no logical truth is without an *a priori* derivation of its truth." Its third root is *mathematical*, which is, for Schopenhauer, a geometrical demonstration, and can be stated as "no theorem is without a geometrical proof." The fourth root is said to be *moral*, by which he does not mean ethical, instead he uses 'moral' to refer to the explanation of actions, both animal and human, in terms of their motives. This fourth root can be stated as "no human or animal action is without a motive." I am inclined to interpret Schopenhauer somewhat differently.

As I see it, what Schopenhauer is saying is that there is just one principle of sufficient reason. He recognizes that it has had a long history in philosophy, in the works of Plato, Aristotle, various Stoics, Sextus Empiricus, Descartes, and Spinoza. But, it is Leibniz that he credits with being "the first to make a formal statement" of it "as a main principle of all knowledge and science."[3] He credits Wolff, however, with being the first to separate the two main meanings of the principle in question. On my interpretation, the principle of sufficient reason should be formulated as "nothing is without an explanation," or to put it more formally, "It is not the case that there exists any x such that x cannot be explained." The four roots can then be viewed as simply four different instantiations of the principle in question. The first root instantiates the word 'nothing' as 'no physical thing' and the word 'explanation' as 'cause,' which yields what was *the first principle of sufficient reason* on the previous interpretation. Likewise, on my interpretation, *the second principle of sufficient reason*, as stated in the previous paragraph, would result if we instantiate 'nothing' as 'no logical truth' and 'explanation' as 'an apriori derivation of its truth.' The third results from instantiating 'nothing' as 'no theorem' and 'explanation' as ''geometrical proof,' and the fourth from replacing 'nothing' and 'explanation', with 'no human or animal action' and 'motive' respectively. This way of interpreting Schopenhauer puts the emphasis where it belongs, namely, upon the epistemological concept of *explanation.*

Schopenhauer credits Wolff with being the first philosopher to distinguish two meanings for principle of sufficient reason, between explanation in terms of causes, and explanations in terms of grounds or reasons, but criticizes him for not clearly defining the difference.[4] Then he discusses Hume and Kant, and concludes with an assessment of the contributions made by them, Wolff, and the other philosophers mentioned previously, regarding the clarification of the principle in question:

> ...it follows as a general result that a distinction was drawn between two applications of the principle of sufficient reason, although this was done only gradually and very tardily, and not without frequent lapses into error and confusion. The one application was to judgments which, to be true, must always have a ground or reason; the other was to changes in real objects which must always have a cause. We see that in both cases the principle of sufficient reason authorizes us to ask *why*, a quality that is essential to it.[5]

Schopenhauer's next step is to argue that recognition of these two meanings of the principle in question is not sufficient. He maintains, as we already know, that there are actually four meanings or roots, and he explains what he means by a root in one of the most informative and important passages in *The Fourfold Root*:

> Our knowing consciousness, appearing as outer and inner sensibility (receptivity), as understanding and as faculty of reason (*Vernunft*), is divisible into subject and object, and contains nothing else. To be object for the subject and to be our representation or mental picture are the same thing. All our representations are objects of the subject, and all objects of the subject are our representations. Now it is found that all our representations stand to one another in a natural and regular connexion that in form is determinable A PRIORI. By virtue of this connexion nothing existing by itself and independent, and also nothing single and detached can become an object for us. It is this connexion which is expressed by the principle of sufficient reason in its universality...this connexion assumes different forms according to the difference in the nature of the objects, such forms being then expressed by a further modification [instantiation] of

22

the principle of sufficient reason, the connexion is still always left with that which is common to all those forms and is expressed in a general and abstract way by our principle [my formulation being "It is not the case that there is any x such that x cannot be explained.] Therefore the relations, forming the basis of the principle... are what I have called the root of the principle of sufficient reason. Now on closer consideration in accordance with the laws of homogeneity and specification, these relations are separated into definite species that are very different from one another. Their number can be reduced to *four*, since it agrees with *four classes* into which everything is divided that can for us become an object, thus all our representations.[6]

The above quote clearly supports my interpretation of Schopenhauer regarding whether or not there is really four distinct principles of sufficient reason. It also emphasizes the importance to his philosophy of the concept of "representation," an aspect of his philosophy that I will eventually have to explicate in the present chapter. When I take up this aspect of his philosophy, I will return to this passage. Schopenhauer devotes a chapter to each of the four classes he mentions in the above quote. In each case, although the principle is regarded in one of its four possible forms, it is revealed to be the "same principle" as "having sprung from the root that is stated here," 'here' referring to the above quote. Should any doubts remain concerning my interpretation, consider what he says much later in *The Fourfold Root*:

> ...I am attempting in this essay to establish the principle of sufficient reason as a judgement having a fourfold ground or reason. By this I do not mean four different grounds or reasons leading by chance to the same judgement, but one ground or reason presenting itself in a fourfold aspect, which I call figuratively a fourfold root.[7]

Before I turn to his discussion of each of his four forms, I want to carefully examine and defend to some extent his contentions about the *a priori* status of the principle of sufficient reason. Schopenhauer claims that the principle of sufficient reason cannot be proven. He claims that Kant and others have attempted to do so, but argues that they were attempting to accomplish the impossible. Every proof, according to Schopenhauer is the "demonstration of the ground or

23

reason for an expressed judgement." To seek a proof for a given proposition is to assume then that a ground or reason for its truth can be given, which is to presuppose the principle of sufficient reason. To seek a proof for the principle itself is therefore to assume it. Or, in other words, Schopenhauer's words, one who seeks a proof for the principle in question "finds himself involved in that circle of demanding a proof for the right to demand a proof."

These remarks of Schopenhauer's will sound familiar to anyone who is conversant with the philosophy of Wittgenstein, for they will remind one of what Wittgenstein has said about "hinge propositions." In *On Certainty*, Wittgenstein says "the *questions* that we raise and our *doubts* depend on the fact that some propositions are exempt from doubt, are as it were like hinges on which those turn."[8] Nowhere in his major work, the *Philosophical Investigations*, does Wittgenstein mention hinge propositions, but his comments there concerning instruments of a language are relevant to this topic. He says:

> There is *one* thing of which one can say neither that it is one metre long, nor that it is not one metre long, and that is the standard metre in Paris.—But this is, of course, not to ascribe any extraordinary property to it, but only to mark its peculiar role in the language-game, of measuring with a metre-rule.—Let us imagine samples of colour being preserved in Paris like the standard metre. We define "sepia" means the colour of the standard sepia which is there kept hermetically sealed. Then it will make no sense to say of this sample either that it is of this colour or that it is not.
>
> We can put it like this: This sample is an instrument of the language used in ascriptions of colour. In this language-game it is not something that is represented, but is a means of representation...What looks as if it *had* to exist, is part of the language. It is a paradigm in our language-game; something with which comparison is made.[9]

A claim like "This is a computer" said when pointing to the one on my desk is a "paradigm of one's language." Such paradigms are instruments of the language-game. Any doubts I might have regarding whether this is a computer on which I am working is hinged upon such instruments or paradigms of the language as "This is a computer" asserted in the presence of a computer. This is why Wittgenstein said on one occasion that the proper answer to such a question as "How do I

24

know that this object in front of me is a table?" would be "I know English." The overall or general language-game, English, depends upon the existence of innumerable hinge propositions of this sort, which is to say it depends upon definitions, and these definitions can be either *ostensive*, as exemplified by my computer case, or *strictly verbal* definitions, which do *not* involve pointing to or other wise indicating that some object present is an example or paradigm of what is meant by the expression being defined.

There are, however, other propositions, non-definitions, which are also hinge propositions and they are much closer to the principle of sufficient reason than are any kind of definition. In his book on G. E. Moore and Wittgenstein, Avrum Stroll makes a distinction that I shall employ, though somewhat differently than he does, namely the distinction between those hinge propositions that are *relevant* and those that are *absolute*. He says:

> ...certitude...stands outside the language game. It does so in two different forms, one relative, and the other absolute. A proposition that is exempt from doubt in some contexts may become subject to doubt in others, and when it does it plays a role in the language game. This is the relativized form of certitude. But some propositions—that the earth exists, that the earth is very old—are beyond doubt; their certitude is absolute.[10]

Definitions, both ostensive and non-ostensive, are relevant in Stroll's sense of the expression 'relevant.' If I were viewing my computer in a smoke filled room I might actually have doubts about whether or not it is a computer, and concede that my ability to offer an ostensive definition is compromised. I am not, however, satisfied with his use of the expression 'absolute.' I do not accept Stroll's example of the earth's being very old as absolute. But there are propositions about which I would be willing to say that they are absolute in Stoll's sense of the term 'absolute,' namely, that they are beyond doubt. There are a number of propositions that James Zartman and I referred to as 'meta-propositions' that are, we argued, immune from doubt.[11] The propositions I am talking about are those that have been singled out by philosophers over the centuries and referred to as "principles," including: the principle of contradiction, PC, which says that one cannot allege both p and not p at one and the same time; the verification principle, VP, which says that no empirical claim can be accepted unless it can in principle be verified; and the identity

25

principle, IP, which requires us to use the same name for the same object in a specific discourse episode. In my book on Moore for this same series, I argued that the scope of these meta-principles, and the practices they formulate is much wider than that of the specific definitions and the practices formulated by them. The meta-principles must also be *adhered* to in order for linguistic communication to be even possible—given that human beings are the way they are. If we were all psychic or had a different kind of brain, such practices might not be necessary. But we are what we are. Just imagine what it would be like trying to communicate with someone who saw no need for factual confirmation, contradicted himself with great frequency, and never used the same expression to designate the same object. Now imagine a group of such people. They would be unable to take any of the initial steps that language formation requires. Unless our actions are in accordance with principles like VP, PC, and IP, we would not be able to talk at all. They are necessary presuppositions for the very existence of natural languages. In the absence of a practice like the one formulated in the dictionary regarding the word 'democracy,' all that follows is that we would be unable to talk about democracies. One way to mark the difference between the two kinds of hinge propositions I have distinguished would be to distinguish between those which are *hinged to specific topics*, and those that are the *hinges upon which any discussion depends.*[12]

Schopenhauer's view that the principle of sufficient reason is *a priori* can be defended as one of those "hinges upon which any discussion depends." In point of fact, Schopenhauer considers the second instantiation of the principle of sufficient reason to be a fourth member of the so-called "laws of thought."[13] The other three are PC, IP, and the law of the excluded middle.

In the chapter Schopenhauer devotes to the second instantiation of the principle of sufficient reason, there is a discussion of four kinds of truth. One of these kinds of truth is "metalogical truth." And in the section of the chapter under consideration concerned with this species of truth he recognizes that there is lack of agreement concerning the number of the laws of thought, but alleges that there are four, and in fact only four, such "judgments of metalogical truth." He formulates the forth "law of thought" as "Truth is the reference of a judgement to something outside it as its sufficient ground or reason." Brian Magee interprets this as the principle "that truth corresponds to reality."[14] Understood in this way, the fourth law of thought sounds very much like an epistemological, rather than a semantic formulation of the

26

verification principle. Although Wittgenstein himself never stated the verification principle in the *Tractatus*, he came close to doing so when he said, "…in order to say "p" is true (or false) I must have determined under what conditions I call "p" true, and thereby I determine the sense of the proposition." (Tractatus, 4.63). In spite of the fact that this formulation appears to promote truth conditional semantics rather than verificationism, one can, as does Peter Hacker, argue that although Wittgenstein certainly did provide a truth-conditional account of the meaning of molecular propositions like, "a is red and b is green," he certainly did not do so for elementary propositions like, "a is red." The truth and meaning of a molecular proposition, for the *Tractatus* Wittgenstein, is simply its truth conditions. Our example would be true only when "a is red" is true, and "b is green" is also true.[15] The truth of an elementary proposition depends, however, on some factual situation in the world. According to Hacker, it "seems likely that the idea of an *elementary* proposition which is not verifiable would not have been intelligible to" Wittgenstein—that "implicit in the *Tractatus* was a commitment to verifiability as a criterion of empirical meaningfulness for elementary propositions, although not a verificationist *definition* of meaning in terms of the method of verification."[16]

To the extent that Hacker is right, and I am in full agreement with him on this issue, there is a remarkable similarity between Wittgenstein and Schopenhauer on this matter. But whether one should consider the verification principle to be a separate principle from the principle of sufficient reason, or to be simply an instantiation of it is an issue that I cannot resolve here.

About the "four laws of thought" Schopenhauer makes this further observation:

> Through a reflection, which I might call a self-examination of the faculty of reason, we know that these judgements are the expressions of the conditions of all thought and therefore have these as their ground. Thus by making vain attempts to think in opposition to these laws, the faculty of reason recognizes them as conditions of the possibility of all thought. We then find that it is just as impossible to think in opposition to them as it is to move our limbs in a direction contrary to their joints. If the subject could know itself, we should know those laws *immediately*, and not first through experiments on objects, i.e., representations.[17]

The last sentence in the above quote involves a claim about

27

representation that will be important later. At any rate, it is clear that, for Schopenhauer, the principle of sufficient reason, PSR, can be understood as a hinge proposition of the kind I referred to in the quote on page 26 above as "hinges upon which any discussion depends." However, it is important that we understand that for Schopenhauer no principle is *intrinsically* true. He claims that the idea or conception of intrinsic truth is really a contradiction in terms. Instead, he maintains "every truth is the reference of a judgement to something outside it."[18] Perhaps what he means by this is that although it is senseless to claim to know *that* VP, PC, IP, PSR, and any other such foundational principles are true, yet knowing *how* to speak a natural language presupposes adherence to them. What Wittgenstein says in (403) of *On Certanty* is in keeping with this idea. He says:

> To say of man, in Moore's sense, that he knows something; that what he says is therefore unconditionally the truth, seems wrong to me—It is the truth only inasmuch as it is an unmoving foundation of his language games. (p. 52e)

It would, I think, be wrong to claim to *know that* such propositions as VP, PC, IP, and PSR are true. I also agree that the proper way to characterize this sort of knowing is as *knowing how*. And, Stroll is probably right that "it is Wittgenstein's main thesis in *On Certainty* that what stands fast is not subject to justification, proof, the adducing of evidence or doubt and is neither true nor false."[19] I disagree, however, with the view Stroll attributes to Wittgenstein. If I am right, and there are practices that we can and do formulate as meta-principles, which *are* necessary presuppositions for the very existence of a natural language, that fact itself constitutes a *justification* of them. It would seem to me hard to imagine a stronger or more significant form of justification than this. Hinge statements of the sort I explicated in terms of the "standard metre" kind of case, namely, definitions, both ostensive and otherwise, are as much subject to changing standards as is what constitutes or measures a metre. Wittgenstein himself allows that "when language-games change, then there is a change in concepts, and with the concepts the meanings of words change."[20] So, although no single hinge statement of the "standard metre" kind can be justified as being a necessary presupposition for the existence of a natural language, VP, PC, and IP can, and, I suspect, so can PSR.

At this point, I want to return to consideration of each of Schopenhauer's four instantiations of PSR I will not, however, give each of them equal time. Schopenhauer himself allots very little space to the last two. I will follow his lead. The third instantiation concerns geometry and mathematics, and Schopenhauer's account of their universality and truth is provided in terms of the *a priori* categories of time and space. It is pure Kant. The fourth instantiation involves motives as explanations of human action, and it does involve ideas that are at the heart of Schopenhauer's major work—*The World as Will and Representation*. Unfortunately, his account of this aspect of his philosophy in the *Fourfold Root* is too brief to be of much use. I will only outline the contents of this segment of the work under consideration. I will elaborate upon it when I turn to Schopenhauer's ethics in Chapter VI of the present work. Here I will emphasize the first instantiation—nothing physical is without a cause.

About his views on causation, most commentators are united in their praise. Taylor says of this part of the *Fourfold Root* that it is where "this work makes its greatest contribution to philosophical thought."[21] There is at least one critic, however, who is an exception to the rule. D. H. Hamlyn concedes that Schopenhauer does offer "some interesting considerations about the nature of causality and the connection between that notion and those of objects and matter," but he goes on to describe the analysis of the first root as a "disaster."[22] I will, after I have explicated Schopenhauer's account of causality, return to and examine Hamlyn's critique of it.

The first step in my analysis of Schopenhauer's views on the concept of "causation" is to explicate its intimate connection with the concept of "representation." I promised to return to this topic on page 23 above, after quoting Schopenhauer's claim that all knowledge is knowledge of representations. To be an object of knowledge is, for Schopenhauer, to be a representation. To claim this is, of course, to adopt Kant's transcendental idealism. Schopenhauer will eventually differentiate himself from Kant by allowing for knowledge of the-thing –in-itself, which identifies with will or ceaseless striving. I will investigate and explicate this aspect of Schopenhauer's philosophy in the next chapter. At the present time, we need only understand that causation for Schopenhauer is defined as a relation between representations, and not between things-in-themselves. And, as he says in the relevant quote on pages 22-23 above, "all our representations stand to one another in a natural and regular connexion that in form is determinable A PRIORI." Now we are in a position to be able to understand his views regarding causation, the central ideas of which can be briefly stated as follows, but first consider his example of a causal sequence of events:

> If a body ignites, this state of burning must have been preceded by a state (1) of affinity for oxygen; (2) of contact with oxygen; (3) of a definite temperature. As soon as this state existed, the ignition was bound to ensue immediately, but only at this moment did it ensue. Therefore that state cannot have existed always, but must have appeared only at this moment. This appearance is called a *change*.[23]

Now we can proceed to summarize his views on causation.

> (a) The law of causality, or the principle of sufficient reason as the ground of becoming, is "related exclusively to *changes* and is always concerned solely with these."

> (b) Every effect is a change or state of being and so is its cause.

> (c) The chain of causality, because it is concerned solely with change, is necessarily without a beginning. What is the cause of one change is itself an effect of another change, and so on "*ad infinitum*."

> (d) The connection between cause and effect is a necessary and not a contingent one. Mere constant conjunction is not sufficient.

> (e) Only states come into being and cease to be, objects neither come into being nor cease to be. Matter is said to be indestructible, and a "coming into existence" of "something that had never previously existed" is "an utter impossibility," "absolutely inconceivable." He refers to this requirement as a "corollary of the law of causation" and dubs it "the law of permanence of substance."

> (f) What we commonly think of, as the "coming into being of a new thing" is really only a change in something that previously existed.

> (g) Causes are not simple states or changes, but are complexes of various states, each member of which he refers to as a "causal condition."

(h) It is a "matter of indifference in what chronological order" the complex set of changes (the "entire causal state") necessary for a specific change coalesce.

(i) A body's state of rest or motion must persist "throughout endless time without change...unless a cause supervenes which alters or abolishes it." Schopenhauer refers to this requirement also as a "corollary of the law of causality," and he names it "the law of inertia."

(j) (e) implies that matter remains unchanged and thus is not subject to the law of causation. There is one other thing that remains unchanged and that is the "primary forces of nature." They are unchanged "because they are that by virtue of which changes or effect are at all possible, that which first gives to causes their causality, i.e., the ability to act."[24]

Another corollary of (e), one that is different from the *law of permanence of substance*, is that it is utterly impossible to prove that God exists by use of the so-called "cosmological proof." This proof argues that given the indisputable fact that there causal change in the universe, we can avoid an infinite regress only if we assume that there is an unchanged cause, namely, God. This proof, two forms of which constitute two of St. Thomas Aquinas's five ways of proving God's existence, would not, even if it were valid, establish that this unchanged Changer is in any way benevolent, or even conscious or aware of what it does. The proof's unchanged Changer could be either malevolent or indifferent or both. But if Schopenhauer is right, this alleged proof is completely fallacious, and there can be no *sensible* questions concerning the properties or characteristics of the unchanged Changer. And the reason for this is that an unchanged Changer is inconceivable. Change requires change, and can only occur if there has been previous change. To be a changer is to be what has been changed. In Schopenhauer's philosophy, the concept of "an unchanged Changer" is a contradictory one.

Schopenhauer goes on to claim that the principle of causality is manifested in nature in "three forms:" physical causes; stimuli; and motives. They differ only, however, in terms of the "degree of *receptivity* or *susceptibility* of beings, the greater this is the lighter can be the mode of operation, thus a stone must be kicked, whereas a man

31

obeys a glance." A motive is just a cause that "passes through knowledge." The intellect is said by Schopenhauer to be "the medium of motives. But a motive is no less a cause because of the non-physical nature its medium. Motives operate with the same necessity as do physical causes. Does this mean that there is no freedom of the will? Yes and No. Schopenhauer has a unique and interesting position on that ages old problem known as the freedom of the will problem.

For Schopenhauer, the human intellect has a dual nature. The intellect consists of knowledge of "intuitive perception," but it also consists of "abstract knowledge." The first is bound up with the present. For Schopenhauer, experience is not simply sensation. It is one thing to have a sensation of a given representation, it is another thing to know what that thing is, say a tree. To see the given phenomena as a tree involves the intellect or understanding. Seeing a tree, which is only possible to do at some presently existing moment in time, is an act of intuitive perception. Abstract knowledge, on the other hand, involves reason, which is not, according to Schopenhauer, temporally bound. I can perceive that that is a bottle of whiskey that one person offers me, and I can see that another person is offering me a cup of tea. I am inclined to have a glass of whiskey, yet I am motivated also by the desire to overcome my tendency toward alcoholic beverages. I can, or so it would seem, on the basis of these considerations, through the use of reason, balance these "mutually exclusive motives," one against the other, and make a *free* decision as to which course of action to follow. Not so, according to Schopenhauer.

What happens, according to Schopenhauer, is that the stronger motive will of necessity win out, and one's "action ensues with precisely the same necessity with which the rolling of a ball results from being struck." It is the fact that our intellect is twofold in nature that, according to Schopenhauer, creates the *illusion* that freedom of the will exists. In the example I gave, it appears to be the case that "two different actions are possible to a given person in a given situation," and thus that there is freedom of the will. This appearance is the result of intuition or perception. But decision is not reached at that point, but rather by reason, which is itself determined by the strongest motive.

Schopenhauer's philosophy of causation is rather obviously interesting and important. The importance of its implications concerning both the cosmological proof for God's existence and the freedom of the will issue have, I think, been demonstrated. So it would seem that even if Schopenhauer's views on causation are not without fault, they surely do not constitute a disaster. Why does Hamlyn think that they do?

According to Hamlyn, among the topics that are encountered in the section on causality is Schopenhauer's theory of sense perception, which plays an essential role in his "argument for the apriori character of" the principle of sufficient reason as it applies to causality. He credits Schopenhauer with insisting upon the distinction between sensation and perception, but argues that Schopenhauer fails to adequately account for how the principle of sufficient reason, as instantiated for causes, is to be set out in terms of 'how representations are as objects for a subject." As we determined previously, for Schopenhauer everything said about an empirical object has to be interpreted or restated in terms of talk about representations for the subject or the perceiver, which is straight forwardly Kantian. And it is not sensation alone that constitutes perception of an object, but also understanding. It is through understanding that the principle of sufficient reason manifests itself. According to Hamlyn, "if it is true that empirical representations cannot stand alone, but must occur for the subject in an ordered connection according to the principle of sufficient reason," then this is the work of the understanding. But the problem is that, for Schopenhauer, immediate knowledge is only available through inner sense, and inner sense is governed by temporality only. Since, however, Schopenhauer's analysis of causality restricts its application to just those representations that have a spatio-temporal form, it is impossible to see how such objects, those governed by the principle of sufficient reason as instantiated for causality, can be objects for the subject. This is because "as far as concerns the immediate presence of representations in consciousness, the subject remains under the form of time alone." [25] Even if Hamlyn is right about this matter, and I think that he is, his description of Schopenhauer's views on the subject as "disastrous" seems to me to be much too strong. At worst, it constitutes a puzzle that might with effort be unraveled in favor of Schopenhauer. As I suggested previously, the principle of sufficient reason might well be defensible as a necessary presupposition for the very existence of a natural language, particularly its first instantiation. [26]

I want now to briefly discuss the remaining three instantiations of the principle of sufficient reason. The second instantiation of the principle of sufficient reason, which takes as its objects logical truths, and which I formulated above as "no logical truth is without an apriori derivation of its truth," is, according to Schopenhauer, concerned with judgment. He formulates it thus: "if a judgement is to express a piece of knowledge, it must have a sufficient ground or reason." If a belief qualifies, it is then held to be true. There are, however, according to Schopenhauer, four kinds of grounds on which truth can be founded. I have already discussed on page 27 above the kind of ground he considers to be the "metalogical variety." There are, in addition, according to Schopenhauer, three other kinds of truth grounds: logical, empirical and transcendental. Logical truth is the kind of truth that a conclusion has that follows from another truth. In logic, we commonly refer to this kind of grounding of a proposition's truth as soundness. If a conclusion follows from a premise as a matter of form it is said to be *valid*. If, in addition, the premise is true, we say that the argument is *sound*, and that the conclusion must be true. Material or *empirical* truth is the kind of truth that is directly grounded in experience itself. A logical truth can also be materially true. This happens when the truth of the premise of a logical truth is itself grounded in experience. The third kind of truth, namely, transcendental truth, applies to those propositions which Kant labeled *synthetic apriori*. Such judgments are said "to rest not merely on experience, as do material truths, but on the conditions of the entire possibility of experience which lie within us." The whole of mathematics is said to be based upon, or as he puts it, is "evidence of such truths."[27] Another example of such truths is, for Schopenhauer, as it was for Kant, "nothing happens without a cause," which is also the *first* instantiation of the principle of sufficient reason. In addition to being transcendentally true, these truths are also material truths, which is, of course, why Kant called them "synthetic apriori."

Schopenhauer begins his quite brief discussion of the third instantiation of the principle of sufficient reason, which concerns mathematical or geometrical demonstrations, by distinguishing those representations that are its concern from those representations of the first instantiation. In Kantian fashion, he describes the former representations as "representations in which time and space are *pure* intuitions," and the latter as those "representations in which time and space are *sensuously and conjunctly perceived*." He claims that the essential difference between them is matter. Nothing he says in this chapter is importantly different from what Kant held to be true regarding math and geometry. Like Kant, Schopenhauer regards space and time to be pure *a priori* intuitions of outer and inner sense respectively, which is to say that representation in space and time is a precondition of, and not a demonstrable ground of mathematics.

The last class of objects to be grounded in the principle of

34

sufficient reason is the class of human actions. This is what I have referred to as the fourth instantiation of the principle of sufficient reason, which is to say that, of necessity, every human action is explicable or grounded in a motive. But since the objects as represented, are as motives indistinguishable from the subject of the knowing, there is really only one object "the immediate object of the inner sense, *the subject of willing.*" As an object of inner sense it can only be represented in time, and not in space. For Kant, the subject or the "I" is inherent in all representations. A representation cannot exist as unrepresented in the subject. The "I" itself cannot exist as a representation; therefore it cannot exist as an object. But, for Schopenhauer, the subject from within is not a knower, but a willer. We know the will, and thus the willer, directly through inner experience, which does not require the form of space, but only the form of time. "To this extent," concludes Schopenhauer, "the subject of willing" is "for us an object."[28] I will explicate all of this quite carefully in the next chapter.

---

[1] Schopenhauer (1974) p. xxviii.
[2] Richard Taylor (1974) p. x.
[3] Schopenhauer (1974) p. 24.
[4] Ibid., p. 25.
[5] Ibid., p. 39.
[6] Ibid., pp. 41-42.
[7] Ibid., p. 162.
[8] Wittgenstein (1972) sect. 341, p. 44e.
[9] Wittgenstein (1958) sect. 50, p. 25e.
[10] Stroll (1994) p. 138.
[11] Odell and Zartman (1982) pp. 72-74. Odell (2001) pp. 67- 69.
[12] Odell (2001) p. 67.
[13] Schopenhauer (1974) pp. 156-163.
[14] Magee (1983) p. 31.
[15] Where a and b refer to simple objects.
[16] Hacker (1996) pp. 52-53.
[17] Schopenhauer (1974) p. 161.
[18] Ibid., p. 159.
[19] Stroll (1994) p. 138.
[20] Wittgenstein (1972) sect. 65, p. 10e.
[21] Taylor (1974) p. x.
[22] Hamlyn (1980) p .21.

[23] Schopenhauer (1974) p. 53.

[24] Ibid., pp. 52-69.

[25] For details of Hamlyn's critique, which is far too complex to treat in the present work, the reader should consult Hamlyn (1980) pp. 16-21.

[26] This topic is also too complex to treat here. I intend to treat it in considerable detail in a future paper on the topic of hinge propositions.

[27] To review what I claimed was a serious problem with this idea that Schopenhauer borrowed from Kant, see footnote [1] of Chapter II of the present work.

[28] Schopenhauer (1974) pp. 207-211.

IV
The World as Will and Representation

I. The World as Representation

The title to this chapter ought to be "The World as Representation, but ultimately as Will," and the reason I say this is because that title would best describe the key thesis of Schopenhauer's major work, *The World as Will and Representation*. It would also reflect the fact that he *begins* the work in question by arguing for the thesis that the world is representation. Be that as it may, I will proceed, as did Schopenhauer, with an analysis of his thesis that the world is representation, and follow it with an exposition of his thesis that the world is *ultimately* will. It is regarding the will that Schopenhauer departs from Kant and marks his own territory. Kant's unknowable things-in-themselves become transformed into *the* thing-in-itself. And it is this territory that Schopenhauer is most concerned to map in his major work.

Schopenhauer completed *The World as Will and Representation* sometime in 1818. It was published in December of that year. In it he considered himself to have solved "the enigma of the world." He remained convinced of this until his death in 1860. The major thesis of this monumental work is that the world "exists only for the subject." It is pure representation. He considers this idea to be the "one thought" sought by philosophers throughout recorded history. He devotes the entire book to this one thought—all twelve hundred pages of it.

The World as Will and Representation is divided into four books—he has a decided fondness for the number four—each one of which presents a different aspect of the one thought. He regards this work to be an organic whole, where every part supports, and is supported by, every other part. He recognizes, however, that a book belies this conception since every book has a first and a last sentence. To this extent, the form and the actual content of his book are said by him to be in contradiction with each other. In addition to the four books that comprise *The World as Will and Representation*, there is an appendix critical of Kant. In 1844, he published a second edition consisting of two volumes. Volume I was mostly a reprint of the original work. Volume II, a work of fifty chapters subsumed under four headings referring to the four books of the first volume, consists of supplementary, but quite important, material for each of the four books of Volume I. In this chapter, I will discuss each of the first two books of Volume I, and will incorporate into the discussion where appropriate supplementary material from Volume II. At the end of the present chapter, I will discuss the Appendix to Volume I, the subject matter of which is Schopenhauer's critique of Kant. The third book of *The World as Will and Representation*, "The World as Representation: Second Aspect," contains Schopenhauer's theory of ideas or universal forms and his views concerning the nature of art. I will devote my Chapter V to the third book. The fourth book is entitled "The World as Will: Second Aspect." It contains Schopenhauer's ethics, and includes various ideas concerning the philosophy of life. In Chapter VI, I will examine his ethics, and his views concerning the meaning of life.

One commentator has compared *The World as Will and Representation* to a four-act drama—a tragedy.[1] The first act replicates the *Fourfold Root* by explaining how the world of appearance must be understood via the principle of sufficient reason. Act two, the second book, offers details of the various manifestations of the will and reveals its nature. The knowledge gained in the first act leads us to an understanding of will as an impulse that is blind, ceaseless, omnipresent, and insatiable. This leads us to wonder if there can be any salvation, any release from this unquenchable striving that is the essence of human existence. Act three attempts to find in aesthetic contemplation of nature and of life relief from the voracious striving that is our destiny, but the relief gained from artistic contemplation is short lived. The final act offers hope in the form ethics and asceticism, only to frustrate it through scepticism. Human existence is, for Schopenhauer, undeniably tragic.

The first volume's first book, which describes the First Aspect of the one thought, the world as representation, is subtitled "The Representation subject to the Principle of Sufficient Reason: The Object of Experience and of Science." Here he argues that nothing is more certain than the fact that "everything that exists for knowledge, and hence the whole of this world, is only object in relation to the subject, perception of the perceiver, in a word, representation." And, moreover, "this holds good of the present as well as the past and future, as what is remotest as well as what is nearest; for it holds good of time and space themselves, in which alone all these distinctions arise."[2] He asserts that this truth was implicit in the work of Descartes, but that it was Berkeley who was the first to "enunciate it positively." Nevertheless, according to Schopenhauer, the details of Berkeley's doctrines concerning it are to be rejected. He admonishes Kant for having overlooked this truth, and announces that Kant's "neglect" of it is to be the subject of his Appendix. He then praises Indian philosophy, specifically Vedânta philosophy, for having not only recognized this truth, but for having enshrined it as the first tenant of their philosophy. This form of Hindu philosophy has been around for centuries, and Schopenhauer's understanding of it is provided by him in the form of a quote from, "On the philosophy of the Asiatics," by Sir William Jones:

> The fundamental tenet of the Vedânta consisted not in denying the existence of matter, that is, of solidity, impenetrability, and extended figure (to deny which would be lunacy), but in correcting the popular notion of it, and in contending that it has no essence independent of mental perception; that existence and perceptibility are convertible terms. (*Asiastic Researches*, vol. IV, p. 164)[3]

Schopenhauer adds, "these words adequately express the compatibility of empirical reality with transcendental ideality." We must not, however, conclude . from this that Schopenhauer's views were influenced by eastern philosophy. He did not discover it until after the formulation of his own brand of transcendental idealism, which he happily acknowledges was the result of studying Kant.

From the start he hammers home his basic premises. He tells us that there are two sides to the world. On one side there is will, on the other there is representation. Moreover, the subject is defined as that which "knows all things, and is known by none." It is further described as "the supporter of the world," and as "the universal condition of all that appears." Accordingly, "whatever exists, exists only for the subject." Each of us, according to Schopenhauer, "finds himself as this subject, yet only in so far as he knows, not in so far as he is the object of knowledge." Our bodies are objects, and hence representations. Our bodies, unlike other objects, are *known immediately*, but like other bodies they are known through the innate categories of space and time. As such their plurality is necessitated. The subject, the knower, which is never the known, for Schopenhauer, is not subject to the forms or categories of perception. The subject is, however, "always presupposed by those forms themselves." For these reasons, the subject is neither "plurality, nor unity." It is never known, but it is "precisely that which knows whenever there is knowledge." It is "whole and undivided in every representing being." [4] Schopenhauer draws the following conclusions from these considerations:

> Hence a single one of these beings [the subject] with the object completes the world as representation just as fully as do the millions that exist. And if that single one were to disappear, then the world as representation would no longer exist. Therefore these halves [the subject and object] are inseparable even in thought, for each of the two has meaning and existence only through and for the other; each exists with the other and vanishes with it... The common or reciprocal nature of this limitation is seen in the very fact that the essential, and hence universal, forms of every object, namely space, time, and causality, can be found and fully known, starting from the subject, even without the knowledge of the object itself, that is to say, in Kant's language, they reside *a priori* in our consciousness...Now in addition to this, I maintain that the principle of sufficient reason is the common expression of all of these forms of the object of which we are *a priori* conscious, and that therefore all that we know purely *a priori* is nothing but the content of that principle and what follows therefrom; hence in it is really expressed the whole of our *a priori* certain knowledge.[5]

Notice that he is here appealing to our old friend from the previous chapter—the principle of sufficient reason. Schopenhauer, in fact, warns the reader that what he is saying here presupposes knowledge of *The Fourfold Root of the Principle of Sufficient Reason.* Nevertheless, what Schopenhauer is saying regarding the nature of the relation of subject to object is, on the face of it, hard to swallow. That the disappearance of any subject entails that its personal representations will likewise perish is indisputable. But it hardly follows that if a given subject dies that the world as representation would no longer exist. As long as there is even one existent subject in the world, it would seem to follow that the world as represented by that subject would continue to exist. However, if one regards the subject to be one and only one thing, which is commonly misconceived as divisible, then Schopenhauer's declaration is more palatable. Palatable is one thing, however, and pleasing to the appetite is quite another. Since taste is largely alterable—the gag response to yesterday's spinach is replaced today by a palate salivating in anticipation of a mouthful of that same leafy vegetable—Schopenhauer's task is to create in us a taste for exotic and untried delicacies. He must transform and replace our present appetites.

He chooses to begin his conversion of our taste buds by convincing us of the importance of the principle of sufficient reason. Since we have already been over this ground in the previous chapter, we need only consider what he *adds* to our understanding of it in *The World as Will and Representation.* Hamlyn, rightly I think, recognizes at least one important additional point, namely, "that one should avoid attributing the relation between cause and effect, which must hold good of the changes that we find in representations, to the relation between subject and object also."[6] This is an important consideration for Schopenhauer because, according to Hamlyn, if one *does* attribute the causal relation to exist between subject and object, this "leads to what he [Schopenhauer] calls 'realistic dogmatism' (that there really is an object quite separate from the subject and the representations that exist for it) and scepticism (that we can never know of any real being that lies behind representations)."[7] For Schopenhauer, the first instantiation of the principle of sufficient reason only applies to representations.

Schopenhauer continues the section under consideration by interjecting some rather interesting ideas concerning that old philosophical nemesis, which was made omnipresent by the work of Descartes, namely "the dream argument." The question that Descartes posed is, "Since dreams can be extremely realistic, how can we ever be sure that we are not dreaming?" Or as it is sometimes put, 'Is there any criterion sufficient to enable us always to know whether or not we are dreaming?" Some philosophers have argued that dreams and waking states are qualitatively indistinguishable, others, including J. L. Austin, have denied this. Austin claims that we are all aware of the fact that dreams are qualitatively different from waking states, that the former unlike the later are characterized by an elusive "dream-like quality," which writers, painters, and other artists try unsuccessfully to capture in their work. He argues, "If dreams were not 'qualitatively' different from waking experiences, then *every* waking experience would be like a dream; the dream like quality would be, not difficult to capture, but impossible to avoid."[8] Schopenhauer disparages the debate itself, and he does so in the spirit of Frank Ramsey's meta-philosophical position concerning philosophical debates, namely, that on-going philosophical debates often turn on a shared, but false, presupposition. Schopenhauer claims that the debate in question is based upon the false assumption that one can compare the dream experience with the waking one. One can, according to Schopenhauer, only compare dream *recollections* with the waking state.

Schopenhauer maintains that the only "certain criterion" on which we can rely is "the wholly empirical one of waking." It is only in the *empirical domain* that a causal connection (which as we know on the basis of our study of the *Fourfold Root*) can obtain. It is here that the causal connection "between the dreamed events and those of waking life is at any rate positively and palpably broken off."[9] He credits Kant with having put the matter right, but adds a "metaphor" of his own:

> Life and dreams are leaves of one and the same book. The systematic reading is real life, but when the actual reading hour (the day) has come to an end, and we have the period of recreation, we often continue idly to thumb over the leaves, and turn to a page here and there without method or connexion. We sometimes turn up a page we have already read, at others one still unknown to us, but always from the same book. Such an isolated page is, of course, not connected with a consistent reading and study of the book, yet it is not so very inferior thereto, if we note that the whole of the consistent perusal begins and ends also on the spur of the moment, and can therefore be regarded merely as a larger single page.[10]

Schopenhauer explicates this dream metaphor of his by claiming that dreams:

do not fit into the continuity of experience that runs constantly through life, and waking up indicates this difference, yet that very continuity of experience belongs to real life as its form, and the dream can likewise point to a continuity in itself. Now if we assume a standpoint of judgement external to both, we find no distinct difference in their nature, and are forced to concede to the poets that life is a long dream.[11]

What Schopenhauer is saying is that we have no trouble discerning dreams from waking states because *waking from* dreams itself is the criterion that distinguishes them. It announces to us that we have been dreaming. However, such announcements can themselves be imparted in dreams. We can dream that we are waking, and that is how a dream can point to "a continuity in itself." Theoretically or in the abstract, when there is no empirical issue regarding whether or not one is dreaming, comparison between the continuity of experience presented by both kinds of case reveals no significant difference, and thus, at this level of comparison, we are forced, according to Schopenhauer, to concede the possibility that life is just a dream.

In Volume II, in his supplementary comments to the first book of Volume I, he further defends transcendental idealism's identification of the subject and the object, and relates his ideas on this subject to his views regarding dreaming. He claims that the world as representation is "a phenomenon of the brain." He argues for the identification of the world as one's own representation, by arguing that the world is 'akin to a dream." He argues, "the same brain function that conjures up during sleep a perfectly objective, perceptible, and indeed palpable world must have just as large a share in the presentation of the objective world of wakefulness."[12] The brain function in question is for Schopenhauer the intellect. Since the content of perception, the world, as sensed and interpreted by the *intellect*, and the dream content, are indistinguishable intellectually speaking, and since the former is indisputably a subjective representation, so must the latter be. The object is the representation of the subject, what is real and what is ideal are the same, and transcendental idealism is the only coherent metaphysics. From this perspective, the theoretical question concerning whether or not the whole of life might be a dream is revealed to be empty. Reality is just what it is represented as being.

There is, however, another way of putting the point about our inability to discern a difference between a waking state, and a dream state—one that has consequences regarding the empirical issue of whether or not one is dreaming. When I was a graduate student, I was forced to teach an introductory course in philosophy at eight o'clock in the morning. At that time in my life I suffered from insomnia and rarely slept before three a.m. I had to get up by six a.m. to make my eight o'clock class. After a few weeks, I started to dream that I was up, shaved, and ready to set off for class. I would then wake to discover that I was in bed and that I still had to get up, shave, etc. It was a very painful experience. After a few more weeks, the content of my dreams became more and more extensive. I eventually started dreaming that I was up, dressed, shaved, in my car, at the campus, in my classroom, teaching my classes, even pinching myself to see if I were really awake. I even started to dream that I had done everything I could think of to be sure that I was awake, only to wake and find that I was still in bed. Then I started dreaming that I had awakened to the disappointment that I was still in bed, that I then actually got up, shaved, etc., and then, to my ever increasingly painful disappointment, I would wake up. Eventually I reached the point where I would lie in bed and wonder if I was actually awake. In opposition to Schopenhauer, I was not, while still in bed, "assuming a standpoint external to both" dreaming and waking. There was nothing theoretical, no purely intellectually detached speculation whatsoever, about my inability to determine whether or not I was dreaming. It was a purely *factual* matter, and it factually called into question my usually reliable empirical criterion, namely, that of waking from a dream.

Much of the supplement to the first book is concerned with meeting various kinds of objections that have been or could be raised against transcendental idealism. One of the "principle objections" to it, which Schopenhauer deals with in the supplement to the first book, concerns the subject's being an object for another subject. Since I can be the object (a representation) of another person's consciousness, and since I can know that I exist when he is not perceiving me, does it not follow that it is false that an object can only exist as a representation of a subject? Moreover, since all other objects stand in the same relation to his intellect as I do, can they not also exist independent of his representing them? Schopenhauer answers this objection thus:

> That other being, whose object I am now considering my person to be, is not absolutely *the subject*, but is in the first instance a knowing individual. Therefore, if he too did *not* exist, in fact, even if there existed in general no other knowing being except myself, this would still by no means be the elimination of the

44

subject in whose representation alone all objects exist. For I myself am in fact that subject just as is every knowing being. Consequently, in the case here assumed, my person would certainly still exist, but again as representation, namely in my own knowledge.[13]

What Schopenhauer seems to be saying here is that in my act of perceiving or apprehending the possibility that I might exist independent of a subject or knowing consciousness, I am as a knowing consciousness perceiving myself, and therefore that my being is still dependent upon its being a representation—a representation of mine. Obviously, it is *logically impossible* for me to perceive something without my perceiving it, but this empty tautology in no way shows that the world as such or in itself does not exist independent of perception. It is certainly true that *the way* that humans sense, perceive, and cognize about the world could not exist unless humans exist. But this does not at all preclude the world's remaining as it is after all humans have perished. Other beings with different categories of perception and intellect might very well remain in the universe and their representation of it would, of course, be different. Suppose Rembrandt, Van Gogh, and Picasso, had in fact all painted a "portrait" of Cleopatra based upon a statue of her. Rembrandt's portrait of her will be a radically different representation of her than will those of the other two, and their respective portraits (representations) will radically differ from the portraits of each other, and from Rembrandt's. Looking at these paintings, one would, if he did not know better, never suspect that they were supposed to be paintings of the same subject. Yet the statue continues to exist, and, moreover, had it not had an existence independent from the existence of the representations of the artists in question, my thought experiment would be *inconceivable*. The very concept of "a representation" implies the independent existence of that which is represented.

Someone might object to my objection by pointing out that the subject of the various representations of Cleopatra in my case was itself another artist's representation of her.[14] Is not a statue of her a representation? Yes! But, so what? All I need do is change the example and let the subject be Mount Everest. I choose the example that I did purposefully. It was meant to illustrate just how unimportant is the fact that what is represented is itself a representation. Further consideration of this matter will resurface later after we have considered what Schopenhauer has to say about the will and about painting. It is time to turn to the second book of Volume I, and to its supplemental material in Volume II.

II. The World as Will

Schopenhauer subtitles the second book, "The Objectification of the Will," and thus reveals what he conceives to be his primary task in this part of *The World as Will and Representation.* Near the beginning of the book under consideration, he tells us "the subject of knowing, who appears as an individual only through the identity with the body...is given in two entirely different ways." He then describes these two different ways. "It is given in intelligent perception as representation, as an object among objects, liable to the laws of these objects. But it is also given in a quite different way, namely as what is known immediately to everyone, and is denoted by the word *will.*" He elaborates this idea as follows with respect to any "subject of knowing":

> Every true act of his will is at once and inevitably a movement of his body; he cannot actually will the act without at the same time being aware that it appears as a movement of the body. The act of the will and the action of the body are not two different states objectively known, connected by the bond of causality; they do not stand in the relation of cause and effect, but are one and the same thing, though given in two entirely different ways, first quite directly, and then in perception for the understanding. The action of the body is nothing but the act of will objectified, i.e., translated into perception...the whole body is nothing more than the objectified will, i.e., will that has become representation...Every true, genuine, immediate act of will is also at once and directly a manifest act of the body; and correspondingly, on the other hand, every impression on the body is also at once and directly an impression on the will. As such, it is called pain when it is contrary to the will, and gratification or pleasure when in accordance with the will.[15]

Although it *may* be true in some sense that acting in a certain way involves an act of will, Schopenhauer seems to be obviously mistaken when he claims that every act of will is at once an act of the body. Ordinarily, when we talk about willing and acting, we distinguish them. Wanting or wishing that I had a new Lexus is one thing. Buying a new

Lexus is another thing entirely. There are a variety of good reasons why I do not go out and buy a new Lexus in spite of the fact that I want one. Schopenhauer attempts to overcome this difficulty by distinguishing between willing and *deliberating*. Willing for him can only occur simultaneously with acting. They are the same thing. If I hesitate, I am not willing, but only deliberating about what I will do in the future. Deliberation is an employment of reason. He says, "Only the carrying out stamps the resolve; till then, it is always a mere intention that can be altered; it exists only in reason, in the abstract. Only in reflection are willing and acting different; in reality they are one."[16] On Schopenhauer's account of willing and acting, my willing and acting are inseparable—this is the *objectification* of will.

Motive and action *may* not stand in the relation of cause to effect, but they do, for Schopenhauer, stand in a relation grounded on the principle of sufficient reason, as we determined in the previous chapter. If we restrict the notion of cause and effect, as he does, to physical causes, we can perhaps say as he does that will and bodily action do not stand in the relation of cause and effect. But the fact remains that my intention to raise my arm is, if not the cause of my doing so, nevertheless its *explanation*. But if so, then how can he say that will and bodily action are one and the same. It clearly makes no sense at all to *explain* one thing in terms of what it is identical with. The explanation of something, its cause, reason, or motive cannot be said to be identical with that something; otherwise, we would not be able to make much sense out of Schopenhauer's doctrine concerning the fourfold nature of the principle of sufficient reason.

The only way out of this dilemma is to recognize that what Schopenhauer means by the word 'will' is not what we ordinarily mean by the word in question. We ordinarily use it to mean resolve, determination, desire and motive. None of these ideas are compatible with what Schopenhauer is saying about the will. Anyone can be resolved, determined, motivated, or desirous of what he or she knows she cannot have, and recognizing this, refrain from acting to acquire the object of such desire. Schopenhauer is not, however, using the word 'will' in the ordinary way. Instead, he is using it to mean something like an impulse. But, even the meaning of 'impulse' has to be adopted to meet Schopenhauer's insight since we do ordinarily also describe ourselves as sometimes conquering our impulses, which implies that not every impulse is identical with some action. If we focus on animals, we can better understand how willing can be identical with or inseparable from acting to gain an objective. As far as we know, animals do not entertain various choices open to them, and then decide which course of action to pursue. They appear to immediately put their desires into practice. Animals act impulsively, i.e., without thinking. They follow their instincts. Such impulses as are manifested in animal behavior might best be described as "blind impulses." If we take Schopenhauer to mean by 'will' *blind* impulse, we can resolve our dilemma, and take seriously his contention that the will is not something that can be conquered. Understanding the will in this way will also make it easier for me to explain in the next two chapters Schopenhauer's views regarding the importance of art and asceticism— that they constitute the only means we have for achieving a satisfactory, if not happy, existence.

It might appear to the reader that Schopenhauer's identity thesis regarding will and action commits him to some form of behaviorism. But this would be a mistaken impression, as mistaken as the impression some philosophers have that Wittgenstein is a behaviorist. Schopenhauer's view regarding the identity of willing with the corresponding bodily action of carrying out what is willed is suggestive both of the later Wittgenstein's, and Gilbert Ryle's, anti-Cartesian, anti-cognitivism views. And this connection between Schopenhauer and these philosophers is by no means fortuitous. Both philosophers read Schopenhauer in their formative years.[17] On the Cartesian account, knowing is an "inner" or mental process. No matter what behavior is exhibited by the subject, he doesn't know, for example Gödel's incompleteness proof, unless there occurs in his mind a mental process of knowing the proof. Many contemporary cognitive scientists regard the occurrence of a specific mental process within the mind/brain to be the *cause* of the behavior we identify as providing such a proof. For Descartes, and the cognitivist, unless the subject has the appropriate mental state, nothing he does constitutes his knowing the proof. Wittgenstein attacks this idea in a variety of ways throughout the *Investigations*, and so does Ryle in his *The Concept of Mind*. Ryle refers to the Cartesian view of the matter as the "Ghost in the Machine"—the machine being the body, and the ghost being the mental, or causal accompaniment. Wittgenstein argues that there is no specific mental accompaniment that is always present within the subject whenever the subject knows. One often is under the impression that he knows something when in fact he does not know it. In my graduate student days, when I was taking mathematical logic, I can remember staying up late trying to prove some theorem in Frege's axiomatic system that required many steps. During the night, I would at various times feel quite certain that I could provide a valid proof of the theorem under consideration, but upon trying to put it down on paper, I would discover that I could not, as yet, do so. Sometimes, I would have this same feeling of certainty (mental process) again at a later time only to find that not only did I not yet have a valid proof, but that my mistaken insight at this time was the same one I had had earlier on. Eventually, I would get the same feeling of knowing how to provide the proof when I in fact was able to do so. This kind of case illustrates the contention of Wittgenstein, Ryle, and originally Schopenhauer, that bodily action is just another way of looking at, the other face of, so-called "inner experience."

Few philosophers have accused Wittgenstein of being a radical behaviorist, which is the view that inner states like believing, knowing, feeling, willing, etc. are simply illusions—that they are non-existent. There is no evidence that Wittgenstein ever held such a radical view. In fact all the evidence is to the contrary. Many contemporary philosophers have, however, accused Wittgenstein of being a logical behaviorist. A *logical behaviorist* is someone who holds the view that talk about inner experiences can be reduced to talk about behavior and being disposed to behave in certain ways, but that talk about the latter cannot be reduced to talk about the former. There are some passages in the *Investigations* that are ambiguous enough to support this view. In response to an imagined accuser's question, "But you will surely admit that there is a difference between pain-behavior accompanied by pain and pain-behavior without any pain?" Wittgenstein replies, "Admit it? What greater difference could there be?"[18] The imagined accuser persists, "And yet you again and again reach the conclusion that the sensation itself is a *nothing*." To which Wittgenstein replies, "Not at all. It is not a something, but not a nothing either! The conclusion was only that a nothing would serve just as well as something about which nothing could be said. We have only rejected the grammar that tries to force itself on us here."[19] It is easy to understand how someone not sufficiently familiar with the whole of the *Investigations* might construe what is alleged here to be an instance of logical behaviorism. But is what he has said here enough to make him a logical behaviorist? If not, would what Schopenhauer has maintained about the objectification of the will be sufficient to make him one?

The answer to the first question is no. P.M.S. Hacker defends Wittgenstein's contention "that there must be behavioural criteria for what we call the 'inner,'" by arguing that it "was not an attempt to *preserve* that venerable picture by devising a new logical relation between two distinct domains, the one merely bodily behaviour and the other consisting of ethereal objects, events and processes in the mind."[20] I agree with Hacker's interpretation of Wittgenstein. I understand Wittgenstein to be saying that we *misspeak* when we talk about knowledge of other minds as somehow insufficient, when we adopt skepticism, or alternately, behaviorism of any sort—logical or otherwise. All we are justified in concluding is that we cannot be directly aware of the contents of another person's mind, but to conclude from this that we cannot know what another person is thinking, feeling, or what his beliefs are is like saying that we cannot know what going on behind closed doors in the next room. Suppose a brass band is ensconced within and playing a particularly rousing version of one of Sousa's marches. Knowledge and understanding are accomplishments. If they can be said to refer to anything, what they refer to is not some inner process, but some episode involving a person, a context, and a practice of describing this kind of occurrence as a specific kind of achievement. What accomplishment is there to being what one cannot help being? According to Wittgenstein we distort, corrupt, twist, and unravel the meaning of the term 'knowledge' when we philosophize in the traditional manner. Genuine understanding can only be acquired by focusing upon what we actually say, by exposition of the actual practices that surround a word's use. Wittgenstein provides us with a different perspective on philosophical perplexities, and thereby attempts to silence those inner voices that drive us to seek their solutions. He offers us a unique perspective from which to view philosophical perplexity. His *Investigations* is more than anything else an exposé of skepticism, realism, nominalism, idealism, cognitivism, behaviorism, functionalism, eliminative materialism and all the other venerated isms of philosophy. Ultimately, the problems that philosophy attempts to solve, the problems that dictate choosing between the unsatisfactory isms, are for Wittgenstein pseudo problems.

But how are we to answer the second question? Is Schopenhauer's view really the same as Wittgenstein's, which he no doubt influenced, or is his view really, unbeknownst to him, a form of logical behaviorism? Let us delve a bit further into what he says about the will, especially what he says about our knowledge of it. According to Schopenhauer, as we have seen, our bodies are known to us as representations, and as such are subject to the forms of space and time. They are objects of outer knowledge. Knowledge of the will is, however, inner knowledge, and as such subject only to the form of time. It is known "only in its successive individual *acts*, not as a whole, in and by itself. So, our knowledge of the will or thing-in-itself is incomplete, or imperfect. Still, according to Schopenhauer, this knowledge of it is "far more *immediate* than is any other" kind of knowledge. It is in our acquaintance with one's own will that one becomes acquainted with the "nearest and clearest phenomenon of the thing-in-itself." If every phenomenon, including physical objects like apples, oranges, and pears, could be known as immediately or intimately as one knows the will, we would be "obliged" to conclude that they are not things-in-themselves, but the thing in-itself, namely will. He then informs us that it is in this way that he modifies "Kant's doctrine of the inability to know the thing-in-itself." It is, he tells us, "modified to the extent that the thing-in-itself is merely not absolutely and completely knowable." Nevertheless, it is no longer completely unknown as it is for Kant. It is clothed only under "the lightest of all veils," in so far as one's "intellect, the only thing capable of knowledge, still always remains distinguished from me as the one who wills, and does not cast off the knowledge form of *time*, even with inner perception. What the thing-in-itself is, ultimately and absolutely, remains for Schopenhauer a mystery.[21] On Schopenhauer's account, our knowledge of the thing-in-itself is incomplete, but, according Schopenhauer, his insight that partial knowledge of it is possible is a distinct improvement over Kant's account of it as altogether unknowable.

We can now answer our question concerning whether or not Schopenhauer is a logical behaviorist. He isn't. For him talk about the inner is not reducible to talk about the outer. Conception of and talk about the outer necessarily involves or falls under the forms of space, time, and causality. Conception of and talk about the inner, however, involves only the form of time. Besides, look at what would be lost to Schopenhauer if he were to become a logical behaviorist. Knowledge of his most fundamental and important idea would be lost. The will as the thing-in-itself would have to be sacrificed. The major thrust of his philosophy would be lost. There is no Schopenhauer without the "inner" acquaintance, however limited it may be, of the will or thing-in-itself.

Previously I interpreted Schopenhauer's will as blind impulse. Another concept that seems to fit his conception of the will is "striving." All of us strive to accomplish one goal or another each and every moment of our waking lives. This kind of striving cannot, however, be what Schopenhauer had in mind. For one thing it involves planning and deliberation, and for another it appears to be non-existent in physical objects. Yet, according to Schopenhauer: "In inorganic nature the will objectifies itself primarily in the universal forces, and only by their means in the phenomena of individual things brought about by causes." He says, "metaphysics never interrupts the course of physics, but takes up the thread where physics leaves it," and, "the will is to be recognized primarily" as the "being-in-itself" of the "original *force of nature*." All of which gets summed up as, "the will proclaims itself just as directly in the fall off a stone as in the action of a man."[22]

Brian Magee offers a viable and seductive hypothesis regarding what the will ultimately represents for Schopenhauer. According to Magee, we must "exclude" from our minds what we ordinarily mean by the word 'will' or we will "misconstrue the most central and important doctrines of Schopenhauer's philosophy." He explicates several meanings which Schopenhauer assigns to the word 'will,' but argues that we cannot fully appreciate what he is saying unless we understand the word 'will,' as the thing-in-itself, to refer to "a universal, aimless, undividualized, non-alive force such as manifests itself in, for example, the phenomenon of gravity."[23] Magee finds "massive corroboration" of this reading of Schopenhauer's philosophy in "the whole of biology since Darwin, the whole of psychology since Freud, and the whole of physics since Einstein." Magee's praise of Schopenhauer is extreme, but well argued:

In the fullest scientific sense we now *know* that matter and energy are equivalent; that at the subatomic level the concept of matter dissolves completely into the concept of energy; that every material object is, in its inner constitution, a concatenation of forces and nothing else; and that it is theoretically possible to transform every material object without remainder into the energy that constitutes it. In other words it just is the case that every material object is material object only if regarded in a certain way; and that looked at in another way it is blind force; and that the two are one and the same thing. It is no surprise to learn that the founder of quantum mechanics, Erwin Schrödinger, was consciously and enthusiastically a Schopenhauerian.[24]

I can find nothing in Schopenhauer inconsistent with this interpretation, and I do find a lot to confirm it, particularly those passages I quoted in the first full paragraph on page 48 above. When we take up Schopenhauer's views regarding the meaning of life, I shall again refer to Magee's interpretation of the thing-in-itself.

Schopenhauer's pessimism is nicely explained as a consequence of this interpretation of the thing-in-itself as blind ceaseless energy or force.

I am, however, bothered by the leap that is taken from immediate, but limited knowledge of the will or thing-in-itself through inner awareness to its postulated existence in things external to us, about which we have *no* such knowledge. None of us has any evidence that an apple, for example, has as its thing-in-itself anything like what we experience when we experience our own striving. Take sexual desire, which is something we are all aware of, and which is a ceaseless, energizing force, more or less impossible to resist. It is not certainly not blind. Only certain objects bring it to the surface in our bodies, and into our consciousness. It is a selective force. Physical energy is not selective in this fashion. The transition from the force inherent in sexual desire as directly experienced by me to the force involved in gravity is not an easy one to make. They are as easily perceived as inherently different kinds of force as they are, by Magee's Schopenhauer, to be inherently the same force. Maybe conscious striving is one kind of striving or thing-in-itself, and gravity is another. Nothing in Magee's projection of Schopenhauer's views upon contemporary physics, and their corroboration in the evidence we have in favor of physics, can, with any certainty, carry over into the realm of conscious striving. I do, however, find these ideas of Magee's persuasive, but this is probably only due to the fact that I, like most philosophers, am strongly inclined toward a unified account of any phenomenon, especially the universe. But this is just what Wittgenstein cautions us against. We have to guard against this kind of tendency.

Still, I remain much enamored of a view like Schopenhauer's. I am impressed by it in much the same way I am impressed by a painting by Van Gogh, or Hals, or Picasso, or Rembrandt, or any number of equally great painters. I consider metaphysics to be as the term 'metaphysics,' implies, namely, an intellectual endeavor beyond physics. This is what Aristotle, who coined the expression 'metaphysics' had in mind. As I conceive of metaphysics, its theories are not hypotheses subject to confirmation and disconfirmation. They are not true or false anymore than are works of art. This does not make them less valuable either. That is the major mistake of positivism. Let me illustrate what I have in mind by making a different use of the case of various painters having painted Cleopatra. Van Gogh's painting of her, in contrast to Picasso's, will be more or less equally interesting, worthwhile, thought provoking, and challenging—these are the dimensions appropriate for the valuation or assessment of a work of art. To question whether a given work of art is or is not true is ultimately misguided and inappropriate. I value Schopenhauer's picture of the ultimate nature of things as much on its creative merit as on its scientific merit.

Be that as it may, the reader may feel some uncertainty concerning exactly what Schopenhauer meant to refer to with the word 'will.' I have considered all of the following: desire, drive, impulse, striving, and Magee's view that it is what physicists refer to as force or energy. For Schopenhauer the 'will' is a technical term, yet not one that he defines with the precision demanded by contemporary philosophers. Certain aspects of Schopenhauer's will are clear, however. It is a force, it does manifest itself in the outer world as energy, and it is from the perspective of inner awareness or introspection an irresistible striving or "compulsion." We will learn more about it in the remaining chapters of the present book.

I want now to conclude this chapter by briefly examining Schopenhauer's critique of Kant—the subject of the Appendix to Volume I. He begins his recitation of Kant's failures by lavishing praise upon his subject. He chooses a quote from Voltaire to express, on the title page of the Appendix, his great admiration for Kant, "It is the privilege of true genius, and especially of the genius who opens up a new path, to make great mistakes with impunity." Several pages at the beginning of the Appendix continue in this vein. In fact, the whole of the Appendix is soft in tone.

Although Schopenhauer's critique of Kant is extended over many pages, its essence can be briefly condensed. Schopenhauer claims that Kant's greatest merit was his having made the distinction between phenomenon and noumenon, but that the "great defect of the Kantian system" is Kant's failure to understand that the will is the thing-in-itself or the noumenon.[25] He explains Kant's mistake in terms of his failure to distinguish adequately between percepts and concepts, between *perceptual* knowledge, the acquisitions of sight, hearing, touch, and taste, and *abstract* knowledge, consisting of using concepts, recognizing and applying distinctions, etc. He claims that Kant assumed wrongly that perception involved conceiving, or, in other words, that Kant's account of the "categories" never makes it clear what their role is, whether they are conditions of perception or are restricted to abstract thinking. He accuses Kant of basing his "assumption" of the thing-in-itself upon "a conclusion according to the law of causality, namely that empirical perception, or more correctly *sensation* in our organs of sense, from which it proceeds, must have an external cause." According to Schopenhauer, Kant's law of causality is *a priori* and hence subjective, and sensation, to which we apply the law of causality to infer sensation from its noumenal cause, is also subjective. And since the application of the form of space in which we place the cause of sensation is as a "form of our intellect" *a priori*, it is also subjective for Kant. All of which leads Schopenhauer to claim that Kant's account implies that "the whole of empirical perception remains throughout on a subjective foundation, as a mere occurrence in us, and nothing entirely different from and independent of it can be brought in as a *thing-in-itself*, or shown to be a necessary assumption." Had Kant clearly separated perceptual knowledge from abstract knowledge, as Schopenhauer claims to have done, Kant would have "separated representations of perception from concepts thought merely *in abstracto*." Kant would then have "known with which of the two he had to deal in each case." In summary, on Schopenhauer's account of the matter, if one fails to fully appreciate the differing roles of the intellect and perception, and restricts knowledge of the thing-in-itself to perceptual knowledge—knowledge through outer sense, under the forms of time, space and causality, one will mistakenly conclude, as did Kant, that the thing-in-itself cannot be known. Our knowledge of the thing-in-itself is, according to Schopenhauer, accomplished via the intellect, through concepts that are derived from inner sense, under the form of time alone.[26]

Schopenhauer's efforts to work out a comprehensive, elegant, and unique philosophy based upon Kant's work is, if not true, or even confirmable, nevertheless, one of the great moments in Mankind's intellectual history. Its implications for the possibility of meaningful human existence, which includes a unique perspective on the importance of art, morality, and asceticism—topics that I shall address in the remainder of the present work—are as thought-provoking as any ever proposed.

---

[1] Höffding (1955) p. 221.
[2] Schopenhauer (1969) Vol. I, p. 3.
[3] Ibid., Vol. I, p. 4.
[4] Ibid., pp. 4-5.
[5] Ibid., pp. 5-6.
[6] Hamlyn (1980) p. 64.
[7] Ibid., pp. 64-65.

[8] Austin (1962) p. 49.
[9] Schopenhauer (1969) Vol. I, pp. 16-17.
[10] Ibid., p. 18.
[11] Ibid., p. 18.
[12] Ibid., Vol. II, p 4.
[13] Ibid., Vol. II, p. 6.
[14] Here the subject and the object are *truly* identical!
[15] Ibid., Vol. I, pp. 100-101.
[16] Ibid., p. 100.
[17] See Magee (1983) pp. 286, 287, 314, and Gardner (1967) pp. 169 ff.
[18] This comment is sufficient in itself to show that Wittgenstein was not a radical behaviorist.
[19] Wittgenstein (1958) sect. 304, p. 102^e.
[20] Hacker (1996) p. 254.
[21] Schopenhauer (1969) Vol. II, p. 197-198.
[22] Ibid., p. 299.
[23] Magee (1983) p. 144.
[24] Ibid., pp. 145-146.
[25] Schopenhauer (1969) Vol. I, pp. 413-437.
[26] See Hamlyn (1980) for a detailed exposition and critique of Schopenhauer's critique of Kant, pp. 41-52.

V

The Foundations of Aesthetics: Plato's Eternal Forms

Schopenhauer was one of the more interesting and comprehensive aestheticians in the history of philosophy. He had views concerning the aesthetics of music, the pictorial arts, poetry, and music. More intriguing, however, is the fact that he looked to art as a possible means for coping with the endless striving (the will) that he regarded as the bane of human existence. He devotes the third book of the *World as Will and Representation* to this topic. It is entitled "The World as Representation: Second Aspect." It is here that he pays homage to, and borrows from the other major influence upon his philosophical development, namely Plato, and it is here that he discusses art and its positive implications for a meaningful existence. All of this is made clear by the subtitle of this section, "The Representation Independent of the Principle of Sufficient Reason: The Platonic Idea: The Object of Art."

On the title page he quotes in Greek from Plato's *Timaeus*, but translates it for those without knowledge of Greek as, "What is that which eternally is, which has no origin? And what is that which arises and passes away, but in truth never is?" Plato's answer to the first question is the eternal Ideas. His answer to the second question is the world of becoming—the empirical world. Before we can fully

57

appreciate Schopenhauer's views regarding Plato's Ideas, a bit of stage setting is needed.

Plato's doctrine of the forms is meant to explain or account for the fact that among all the various things we encounter in the world some things so closely resemble other things as to appear to be indistinguishable were it not for their individuality. Take cormorants as an example. If one walks along the craggy seashores of Ireland, one encounters large numbers of black, web-footed birds dive bombing the ocean's surface intent upon spearing their prey—any denizen of the sea small enough for the dive bomber to extract from its watery domicile. It is virtually impossible to distinguish any one of these birds of prey from another. If we capture a dozen or so, and dye their each one of their heads a different color, and name each one, we can then release them, and later recognize and differentiate between our dozen denizens when we walk along the shore. But this is because we have managed to individualize them. Our inability to recognize them independent of our marking them in this or some other way is explained by the existence of Universal forms. They are said by Plato, and all his many historical followers, to be instantiated by each individual, and to account for sameness of species. Moreover, they are said to be eternal and unchanging. They are, according to Keith Campbell, a contemporary Australian metaphysician, who like other contemporary Australian metaphysicians enjoy wrestling with the so-called "problem of universals," "the only, or at least the best, way to solve a manifest problem: the problem of accounting for resemblance among the world's realities, of accounting for the recurrence of repeated characters." He continues:

> Universals are proposed as the solution to the question: what is it, in the ontic structure of reality, that accounts for those facts of orderly resemblance across space and recurrence through time which we encounter? The problem of universals is only secondarily a semantic issue.[1]

.

I am not, however, convinced that the semantic issue is *only* a secondary issue. As I see it, the *ontic* (objects) and *semantic* (words) aspects have been entangled to produce the controversy about universals. Moreover, I think that a semantic focus provides one with the means for resolving the problem of universals, a task to which I will return eventually. It was Plato who, with his talk of beds and tables, justice, beauty and the good, set the stage for all subsequent performances of the drama known as the nominalism/realism controversy, and although his concerns were primarily ontic, look at what he has Parmenides say, and Socrates assent to, regarding the importance of the universal forms for meaningful discourse:

> . . if in view of all these difficulties and others like them, a man refuses to admit that forms of things exist or to distinguish a definite form in every case, he will have nothing on which to fix his thought, so long as he will not allow that each thing has a character which is always the same, and in so doing he will completely destroy the significance of all discourse.[2]

This is the way Plato sees it. There have been many variations on this theme, but all realists maintain that universals exist. What about the competition? What about the nominalist? Well, according to Campbell, there is more than one way to spell 'nominalist'. He says:

> Some writers use the label 'nominalist' for every denial of universals, but this blurs a crucial distinction: ordinary nominalisms, in denying universals, deny the existence of *properties*, except perhaps as shadows of predicates or classifications. They recognize only concrete particulars and sets: in Quine's case, space-time points as well; in Goodman's case, not even sets, let alone properties. But the trope philosophy emphatically affirms the existence of properties (qualities and relations).[3]

The "trope" philosophy is the newest kid on the nominalism/realism block. It is the metaphysical viewpoint favored by the contemporary Australian metaphysicians. Campbell himself spells 'nominalism' with a capitol P, where 'P' stands for property, and a property is a trope, which is simply an abstract particular existing in space and time. But that is not the half of it. The bigger half of the mouthful is that these tropes are it. Nothing else, except space and time, exists![4] What we ordinarily think of as things, diamonds for example, are just bundles of tropes.[5]

Campbell does not, however, view himself as a nominalist in the traditional sense of the word. Traditional nominalists incorporate the realist's belief that qualities or relations must be universals. Campbell cites Frank Ramsey's admonition, which I previously made use of on page 42 above. Campbell expresses Ramsey's view as, "when a philosophical dispute presents itself as an irresolvable oscillation between two alternatives, the likelihood is that both alternatives are false and share a common false presupposition." He then applies it to conclude, "that Realism and Nominalism in the problem of universals exhibit precisely this pattern, their common, false presupposition being that any quality or relation must be a universal."[6] As Campbell sees it, realism is a dualistic account of the nature of things, and nominalism is just one of several possible reductive monisms. Particularism is one of these competing monisms, and tropism is best understood when conceived of as one of its forms. He seems to prefer the label 'Resemblance Nominalism' for his form of trope theory, according to which "the properties of things are themselves particulars, and there are no universals."[7]

D. M. Armstrong, the leading light among the contemporary Australian metaphysicians prefers, however, to be thought of as a realist. Realists can, as he views the matter, be placed within one of two camps: the camp that believes that properties are universals, and the camp that believes that properties are tropes. Both camps are realist camps because they both believe that properties exist. They only differ regarding the nature of these properties. Universal realists believe that properties exist independently of the objects in which they are instantiated; Trope realists believe that they do not.

Campbell and Armstrong are, however, united in their efforts to wed the best of both worlds, realism and nominalism, so as to bring about a solution to the age-old conflict between the two. Campbell credits Donald Williams with the insight needed to resolve the age-old controversy between realists and nominalists. On Williams' account of the matter, the realist is allotted the existence of attributes, the nominalist the non-existence of universals. Attributes, tropes, are said to exist as particulars. To say that two spots are the same shade of green is, on this account, to say that each has is a particular shade of green, and that they greatly resemble one another. Sameness of attribute is no longer recognized to be a matter of identity, and so there are no universals.[8]

The stage is now set for Schopenhauer's entrance upon it. We have prepared the stage both for the exposition of Schopenhauer's account of universals, and for the entrance of his stand on the nominalism/realism issue. It is also set for a critical assessment of Schopenhauer's position on this subject. Let me now delve into

Schopenhauer's account of this issue as it is presented in *The World as Will and Representation.*

Schopenhauer reminds us that he has previously introduced the notion of gradation or *degrees of objectification* of the will—that "there is a higher degree of this objectification in the plant than in the stone, a higher degree in the animal than in the plant." The will's objectification, according to Schopenhauer, "has gradations as endless as those between the feeblest twilight and the brightest sunlight."[9] He asks us to recognize in these grades the Platonic Ideas as "the original unchanging forms and properties of all natural bodies, whether organic or inorganic, as well as the universal forces that reveal themselves according to universal laws." And therefore that these:

> Ideas as a whole present themselves in innumerable individuals and in isolated details, and are related to them as the archetype is to its copies. The plurality of such individuals can be conceived only through time and space, their arising and passing away through causality. In all of these forms we recognize only the different aspects of the principle of sufficient reason that is the ultimate principle of all finiteness, of all individuation, and the universal form of the representation as it comes to the knowledge of the individual as such. On the other hand, the Idea does not enter into that principle; hence neither plurality nor change belongs to it. While the individuals in which it expresses itself are innumerable and are incessantly coming into existence and passing away, it remains unchanged, as one and the same, and the principle of sufficient reason has no meaning for it. But now, as this principle is the form under which all knowledge of the subject comes, in so far as the subject knows as an *individual*, the Ideas will also lie quite outside the sphere of its knowledge as such. Therefore if the Ideas are to become object of knowledge, this can happen only by abolishing individuality in the knowing subject.[10]

The abolishment of which he speaks is accomplished via the affirmation of the thing-in-itself as the knowing subject. He reminds us that he has transformed Kant's paradoxical and obscure thing-in-itself into the will. He announces that Plato's doctrine of the unchangeable forms—his eternal Ideas, is both the most significant doctrine in Plato's philosophy, and also the "most obscure and paradoxical dogma" of Plato's teaching. These Ideas have been, he tells us, "a subject of reflection and controversy, of ridicule and reverence, for many and very differently endowed minds in the course of centuries." He then announces that if we have understood what he has been saying up to this point, we will recognize that not only has he succeeded in making sense of Kant's thing-in-itself, we will be able to follow his argument which concludes that Plato's Ideas are just two sides of the same coin, well, "not exactly identical, but yet very closely related, and distinguished only by a single modification. They are "two entirely different paths leading to the one goal."[11] All of which can be made clear, he says, "with a few words," but what he actually says on this score amounts to far more than a few words. We can, however, simplify somewhat what he wants to say. In doing so, I shall talk about Plato's Ideas rather than, as Schopenhauer does, about Plato's Idea. He does so because his own theory calls for an unindividuated first principle of being. Plato's forms are as numerous as there are kinds of things, even though he does regard the form of the Good as the supreme form

According to Schopenhauer, the Kantian view is that the epistemological forms of knowledge, namely space, time, and causality, belong only to representations, and not to the thing-in-itself. For this reason plurality and change belong only to the will's objectified phenomena. Plato, on the other hand, is viewed by Schopenhauer to have maintained that the empirical world—the world of beds, tables, etc.—has no true reality, it is always becoming. Its constituents are not objects of knowledge. For Plato, only that which is real can be known. Ultimately, Kant and Plato are saying the same thing, namely, that the phenomenal world is meaningless without Kant's thing-in-itself or Plato's Ideas to give it meaning. When we know something, we recognize it and understand what its characteristics are, and it doesn't matter whether there are ten or ten billion of them in the world. All of them can in fact cease to be without in any way diminishing our knowledge of them. It is in this way that Ideas—the universal forms—alone have meaning for Plato. Kant says the same thing by saying that when we perceive a particular thing at a particular time, in a particular space, and as being caused in such and such way, that what we perceive is not a thing-in-itself but a transitory phenomenon. In order to *really* know something, we would have to know it in-itself.[12] For Plato, Ideas, including the form of the Good, can be known, but only in so far as they are directly presented to us, as they are when we pass through the Logos in transmigration from one body to another. For Kant, the thing-in-itself can't be known. Schopenhauer borrows from them both. The thing-in-itself can be immediately known, though not completely, the knower and the known, subject and object, are one. It is, however, as thing-in-itself, as will, not subject to time, space or causality, and thus not *individually* known.

Plato's Ideas as forms as objectification of the will can be perceived in the objects as objectified, and in the perception of them when we perceive their universality and timeless nature as the thing-in-itself. When we view the twilight transformation of our perception of the Atlantic Ocean, what we perceive is an instantiation of the Platonic Idea of such a phenomenon, and the impact it has upon us, aesthetic experience and its timelessness, momentarily frees us from, or at least clouds, the blind, ceaseless striving that is our essence. The contemplation of the form of beauty is for this reason liberating. Unfortunately, it is only a fleeting momentary release from that never satisfied, never abated, underlying striving. Beauty, however, is to be greatly valued for the momentary release it provides, and the work of the artist for the same reason. The artist is a genius who sees and portrays the universal in the particular. The purpose of all the arts, with the exception of Music, is to copy the Ideas, and thereby allow us to contemplate them, by separating them from their phenomenal instantiations as well as the will itself. This is quite paradoxical, however. The will, which is ultimately the subject of all knowledge, must allow itself, which is also ceaseless striving, to be transcended in order to know itself (in contemplation) as timeless, and unchanging. This is, I assume, why such contemplation cannot endure. There are limits to the extent to which these incompatible and conflicting forces can coexist. Since the will is essentially the ultimate reality, it must in the end prevail.

Music is different, however. It allows us access to a copy of the will, not of the Ideas.[13] Music "never expresses the phenomenon, but only the inner nature, the in-itself of every phenomenon, the will itself."[14] For Schopenhauer, the phenomenal world and music are just "two different expressions of the same thing," and music, so regarded, "is in the highest degree a universal language that is related to the universality of concepts much as these are related to the particular things."[15] Nevertheless, neither music nor any of the arts can fully silence "the in-itself of life, the will, existence itself," which is "partly woeful, partly fearful." Art cannot become for anyone, not even the artist, who constantly contemplates the universal in the particular, a silencer "of the will," it cannot "deliver him from life forever, but only for a few moments." We must if we are to find a way to escape from the ceaseless, painful striving that is ourselves, we shall have to seek it elsewhere, namely, "in the case of the saint who has attained resignation," in contemplation of "the serious side of things."[16] This is the subject matter Schopenhauer pursues in the forth and final book of the *World as Will and Representation,* and into which I will delve in the next chapter.

Now, however, I want to question the very foundations upon which rests Schopenhauer's metaphysics of art. I want to question the very existence of universals, or Plato's Ideas. But in doing so I am not going to advocate any form of nominalism to take its place. Nothing anyone, including the Australians, has said on the subject of the nominalism/realism controversy convinces me that it is anything but a pseudo controversy. When philosophers talk about universals and particulars, nominalism and realism, etc., I feel like I have just stepped through Alice's mirror into Wonderland. What I want to do is get us out of Wonderland. Like Dorothy, I want to grab Toto up in my arms, take Alice by the hand, duck out through the mirror, and find Kansas. But how is this to be accomplished? What we need is a map of the linguistic and conceptual terrain.

In the *Investigations,* Wittgenstein cautions us to keep always in mind that the ideas a philosopher forms about the nature of language and meaning will be to some extent formed on the basis of the kind of linguistic example or examples she has in mind when she theorizes. And the likelihood of a reader being convinced by the views a philosopher or thinker expresses will be in part determined by the kinds of examples that pass through the reader's consciousness when he reads or thinks about what the philosopher has said.

There are several different kinds of referring expression, and separating and explicating their differences will help one to understand why focusing on one kind of case while ignoring the others lends credence to mistaken views about the nature both of things, and of the criteria required for correctly using referring expressions.

Among the designating expressions of a natural language like English there are, what I shall call "individuators," terms used to refer to individuals, terms like: 'Sylvia Plath,' 'The person directly in front of me at the present moment,' 'Round Hill, Virginia, 'me,' 'you,' 'this,' and 'that'. Some of these terms are proper names, and some are definite descriptions. Some are personal pronouns, and some are demonstatives. More importantly, some are *descriptive designators,* and some are *non-descriptive designators.* Those that have meaning in the sense of word meaning, and not etymological or associative

64

meaning, are descriptive designators. 'Brave Arrow,' and 'The person directly in front of me at the present moment' are descriptive designators, their constituents are words. 'Sylvia Plath' is a non-descriptive designator. Its constituents are not words. They have no meaning in the relevant sense, although some proper names, like 'Sunny Brown' have extraneous meaning. 'Sunny' is a descriptive adjective, and 'brown' is a color word.[17]

In addition to individuators, there are expressions that are primarily used to refer to kinds of things, but not every such expression is governed by the same considerations. General terms like 'red fox,' and 'Bic Razors' are fundamentally different than general terms like 'game,' 'furniture,' and 'religion'. The former, which I will refer to as *formal abbreviators*, refer to sets of objects, the members of which do possess a number of common features. The latter, which I will refer to, following Wittgenstein, as *family abbreviators*, refer to sets of objects, which do not possess common characteristics but instead possess overlapping and crisscrossing characteristics.

Another and quite different kind of designator is the kind exemplified by 'democracy,' 'justice,' and 'truth'. Here we quite naturally speak of associated concepts. The word 'concept' has a job to do in our language, but its job description does not include its use as a referent for words like 'dog'. Only philosophers talk about the concepts of dog and cat. Dogs and cats inhabit the same world we do. They are not abstractions, and so when we want to inform someone regarding what sort of thing they are, we can simply point to one of them, or to cat or dog pictures. Not so for democracy and justice. Dogs and cats are things, objects. Democracy and justice are abstractions. They are concepts. The words 'Democracy,' 'justice,' 'truth,' etc. are *conceptors*.

If a philosopher focuses on proper names of the non-descriptive designator kind, his vision will be clouded the way Russell's was. Although Russell was concerned with definite descriptions—he provides a theory of them—his thinking concerning the nature of meaning took proper names to be paradigms or models of meaningful expression. Non-descriptive designators are not composed of words, so they have no meaning in the ordinary sense of the word, but they are meaningful, they have reference. Their meanings must, it would appear, be their referents.[18]

A philosopher who focuses on cases like 'the Morning Star' will tend to see things in a Fregian fashion. Such expressions clearly have meaning as well as reference, so one will incline towards the distinction between meaning and reference.[19] If, however, one focuses equal attention on the model proper names provide, one is forced to recognize that many of them have no meaning other than associative meaning, and hence one will not be inclined to accept a theory which incorporates Frege's claims that all expressions including full declarative sentences, are names which possess both a sense and a reference.

The primary reason why some philosophers continue to string along with Plato is that many natural language terms are formal abbreviators—terms like 'cormorant.' These terms and those terms we use to refer to sub-species of our own design, for example, 'German Shepherd,' as well as those terms we use to refer to manufactured items, for example, 'Smith and Wesson 38 special.' are all used to refer to things that exhibit few individual differences. Members of these various classes are extremely difficult to differentiate from other members of the same class. In the case of manufactured items, color can be a help, but only so long as we are just concerned with differentiating between individuals of different color. With the exception of numbers, other mathematical entities, and all other entities whose properties are by definition essential, manufactured items exemplify best the realist's ideal. Athenian beds must have been boringly similar to one another!

Size, a property, and location, a relation, are sometimes all we require for recognition of individual members of classes of natural kinds, breeds, and manufactured items. But often size and location are no help at all. Frequently, we simply cannot tell one member of one of these classes from another member of the same class. In the case of manufactured items, serial numbers are often all we have to go on, but if we are not close enough to read them, they are of no help either. In the case of natural kinds and breeds of our own design, branding or tagging of various sorts is sometimes available to us. But most of the time it is not, as in the case having to do with identifying individual cormorants diving for fish from a cliff side.

When one's focus upon formal designators is coupled with a focus upon conceptors, one is apt to find essentialism irresistible. Focusing on natural species and breeds of human design, with their attendant genetic base manifested in repetitive characteristics, quite naturally leads one to assume that essential characteristics are commonplace. Focusing upon concepts like "justice" and "democracy" leads philosophers to regard essential characteristics as abstractions or forms. Such bifocal vision results in the idea that general terms are not only

66

governed by the existence of essential characteristics, but by ones that are abstract and intangible, even eternal.

On the other hand, a philosopher, like Renford Bambrough, who is captivated by the family type of abbreviator, will embrace anti-essentialism.[20] Family abbreviators are correctly used to refer to sets of objects, the individual members of which manifest with respect to one another quite different, even inconsistent, characteristics. The quest for essential conditions will be seen as a chasing after the wind—vanity and vexation of the spirit. It would be a mistake, however, to conclude from insights founded upon family abbreviators that there is no single thing that can account for correct usage.

There is something which all words do have in common, something which links family abbreviators, formal abbreviators, conceptors etc., to the world. That something is convention! All words are linked to their references, and have their various uses established through specifiable practices. But what is even more significant is the fact that *only* practices or conventions need exist in order for there to be correct and consistent linguistic usage.

If you and I were to *agree* to use the symbol 'toptables,' to refer to those things currently on top of my worktable, it would follow that the coffee cup, the orange peel, the computer, the phone, the lamp, the napkin, and the coffee in the cup are all toptables. There is no single characteristic, or even a set of characteristics these things *all* share. What is important, all-important, is the convention our agreement legislates.

But what about the fact that all toptables are located on my desk? Some philosophers will argue that being on my desk is the essential characteristic for being a toptable. But that would be a mistake. To argue in this fashion is to locate the essential ingredient outside the things, to make relations into properties, and this entails that all things are essentially the same thing. Since everything in the universe could be said to instantiate the relation of being in the universe, everything in the universe would be essentially the same thing. Besides, the spatial and temporal relation used to identify the toptables could as easily have been used to identify a totally different set of objects—objects that are what they are in spite of the fact that they are not on my table.

At any rate, all designators are symbols, and one significant feature that all symbols have in common is that their usefulness presupposes semantic practices—practices that correlate symbols with their referents. Whether or not a given symbol is correctly used is not a question that is answered by determining whether or not the correlated

67

referents possess certain characteristics, but rather by determining whether or not it is used in accordance with a specific practice.

We need not be conscious that we are participating in these practices. We only have to act in accordance with them. Many humans are only vaguely conscious of the existence of such practices or conventions, and could not formulate many of them. This fact does not, however, affect in the slightest their ability to communicate with other humans, and the reason for this is that they *do adhere* to these conventions when they talk. We are from childhood trained to behave in accordance with the semantic and syntactic rules of our respective languages just as we are trained to walk and to ride bicycles. Language use is no more nor less a mystery than are these other accomplishments.

The acquired tendencies or dispositions to use the various symbols of one's language in specific ways are not themselves observable. They have to be inferred, and for this reason they are apt to be misconceived or ignored. We expect there to be something about the objects themselves which cause us to use the symbols the way we do, and so we overlook the practices we have been trained since childhood to follow. These practices or conventions are the primary determinants of correct usage. They guide and direct us toward objects, and they provide the *only* unifying criteria for correct usage. We are only sometimes guided by the similar or identical characteristics objects happen to possess.

The fact that social practices are apt to be overlooked because they are unobservable and intangible may help us to understand why some philosophers find credible Plato's commitment to intangible and unobservable universals. But, it cannot by itself explain why so many of them have followed Plato into the maws of the Logos. I fear the sorcerer's ghost will not be so easily exorcised. We cannot afford to ignore the fact that recognition of sameness *is* essential even for the correct usage of terms like 'toptable' and 'toptables.'

In order for an object which is at the present time on my desk to be identified as a toptable when encountered elsewhere, it will have to be recognized as the [same] object previously present on my desk. That the objects in question are toptables is a matter of convention, and the particular rule that binds them together as toptables is all that is required for them to be called "toptables," but each toptable has to be recognized at subsequent times on the basis of certain properties. It is one thing to say trivially that toptables are called "toptables" because that is what they are called, and another to claim incorrectly that this explains our recognition and identification of a specific individual as a member of the class of toptables.

Have I inadvertently rejuvenated the realist/nominalist controversy? Both the realist and the nominalist would agree that our recognition or identification of these objects as the same ones we had before us when we defined 'toptable' depends upon the existence of certain properties over time. The realist will identify these properties as universals. The nominalist, qua particularist, will insist that they are just those physically existing properties (tropes) we previously encountered. It appears that the nominalist may have the edge here. What is at stake is whether this individual is the same individual we previously encountered, not whether or not this individual has a property or properties that define what it is to be a toptable. We are not concerned with two or more things having the same properties, but only for the same thing to have one property.

Hold on! Wait a minute! We are easing our way back into Wonderland, and before we know it we will be walking with walruses, talking to caterpillars, and otherwise relating to all sorts of never-ever-weres. Happily, we can overcome this obstacle. When we christened them as "toptables," we could have simply put labels of different color and shapes on them, no two of which were exactly the same. By doing so, we make it possible to identify both all the toptables and each particular toptable. These labels facilitate re-identification, but they are not properties, at least not in the ordinary sense of the word 'property,' besides they are all differently colored.

One could, of course, do, as some philosophers are wont to do, and fiat one's way around this conclusion by claiming that being so labeled is itself a property. But we are free to simply reject this claim. We are in no way bound by to accept such adjudications. We could, however, agree to play by the philosopher's rules, agree to abide by his definition of the term 'property,' and then point out that if being labeled in the manner outlined above were to count as a property, this property alone cannot explain our ability to identify the objects on my desk as toptables. It would be no more effective than was the spatial and temporal relation appealed to previously to identify toptables. It could also be involved in the identification of a totally different set of objects. Inter-subjective acceptance of the definition of the term in question, certain visual and auditory clues, a specific sequence of events leading up to and proceeding from the defining of the term 'toptables'—to mention only a few of the relevant contextual parameters—have to occur in order for us to correctly identify individual objects as toptables.

The philosopher customarily plays a game with his own rules, but because he appears to be playing a game with which we are familiar, we are, though confused and perplexed, intrigued, even captivated, by what he claims. Once we realize, however, that the philosopher's game (language, conceptual network, theoretical schema, etc.) is different from our everyday linguistic games: English, French, Spanish, etc., we can either choose to play his game, or we can steadfastly and justifiably refuse to be guided by his rules.

For some philosophers, the fact that the conceptual schema or practices inherent in ordinary language cannot resolve the paradoxes created by philosophers reveals the inadequacies of ordinary language, and thereby demonstrates that it is inferior to practices introduced by the philosopher. These critics of ordinary language are mistaken, however. The rules that govern the philosopher's game are no more relevant to our everyday lives as humans than are those of chess. The restrictions that govern the movement of specific pieces in a game of chess are essentially normative. In reality these pieces can be placed anywhere I choose to place them. Aside from conventional restraints, nothing prevents me from moving a knight anywhere on the board. It is only when I choose to play chess that my positioning of the knights is limited in specifiable ways. And it is only when I play by the philosopher's rules that my notions of certainty, obligation, and of what is or is not real, etc. are seen to be insufficient in any way.

Philosophers who denigrate natural languages, while extolling the virtues of theoretical languages for their superior ability to remove ambiguity and vagueness, fail to appreciate just how adaptable are natural languages. Natural languages contain self-correcting mechanisms, mechanisms for dispelling ambiguities and eliminating vagueness, mechanisms for every increasing precision, mechanisms for adding new words and for redefining any existing word, but these mechanisms are only activated in the context of an actual speech episode, which somehow creates the need for modification. The deficiencies that activate these self-correcting mechanisms do not present themselves in the abstract. They come into play with the emergence of circumstances whose description cannot be accomplished by the vocabulary currently at our disposal.

It is quite proper for philosophers to anticipate possible circumstances that would activate the self-correcting mechanisms of natural languages, and then to suggest vocabulary, which would precisely describe such circumstances. Philosophers are not, however, authorized to adjudicate meanings. The adoption of new meanings is the adoption of new practices and their formulations as rules, and this is accomplished by communities and not by individuals. Individuals can only recommend new procedures for adoption by communities.

With this in mind, we can step back through the looking glass into the familiar world we comprehend and appreciate through natural languages, understanding that we never again need to feel in any way compelled to travel through Wonderland. Let not our complacency blind us to the joys of the open road, however. We all remain free to travel such lands for the sake of intellectual adventures or personal amusement, and to recite our adventures to such kindred spirits as might thereby be inspired to join Plato's and Schopenhauer's caravans. Whatever one thinks regarding the truth of Schopenhauer's metaphysics, one can still appreciate it the way one appreciates a work of art, and base this appreciation upon dimensions different from the true/false dimension. One can ask, for example, is it intriguing, original, coherent, appealing, or consoling?

---

[1] Campbell (1990) pp. 27-28.
[2] Plato (Hamilton, and Cairns ed. 1963) p. 929.
[3] Campbell (1990) p. 27.
[4] Ibid., pp. 3-4.
[5] Ibid., pp. 20-21.
[6] Ibid., p. xii.
[7] Ibid., p. 18.
[8] Ibid., p. 43.
[9] Schopenhauer (1969) Vol. I, p. 128.
[10] Ibid., p. 169.
[11] Ibid., p. 170.
[12] Ibid., pp. 172-173.
[13] Ibid., p. 257.
[14] Ibid., p. 261.
[15] Ibid., p. 262.
[16] Ibid., p. 267.
[17] Odell (1984) pp. 229-231.
[18] Ibid., p. 237.
[19] Ibid., p. 228.
[20] Bambrough (1960).

VI

Pessimism, Morality and Asceticism

The fourth book of *The World as Will and Representation* is devoted to Schopenhauer's moral theory and his philosophy of life. As we determined in the last chapter, Schopenhauer considers the subject matter of this book to be the "most serious side of things." It concerns the actions of men, "the subject of direct interest to everyone, and one which can be foreign or indifferent to none." It is, according to Schopenhauer, what is usually considered to be "practical" as opposed to "theoretical" philosophy. For him all philosophy is really theoretical, but he says he will be discussing what is "commonly referred" to as practical philosophy—philosophy of life issues. To begin, let me emphasize the previously mentioned fact that Schopenhauer's philosophy of life is extremely pessimistic in character. Consider what he says early on in the forth book:

> The life of every individual, viewed as a whole and in general, and when only its most significant features are emphasized, is really tragedy; but gone through in detail it has the characteristic of a comedy...The never-fulfilled wishes, the frustrated efforts, the hopes mercilessly blighted by fate, the unfortunate mistakes of the whole life, with increasing suffering and death at the end, always give us a tragedy. Thus, as if fate wished to add mockery to the misery of our existence, our life must contain all the woes of tragedy, and yet we cannot even assert the dignity of tragic characters, but, in the broad detail of life, are inevitably the

foolish characters of a comedy.[1]

If this passage is not enough to convince one of the darkly pessimistic character of his philosophy, consider the following passages from his *Essays and Aphorisms*:

If the immediate and direct purpose of our life is not suffering then our existence is most ill-adapted to its purpose in the world: for it is absurd to suppose that the endless affliction of which the world is everywhere full, and which arises out of the need and distress pertaining essentially to life, should be purposeless and purely accidental. Each individual misfortune, to be sure, seems an exceptional occurrence; but misfortune in general is the rule.

I therefore know of no greater absurdity than that absurdity which characterizes almost all metaphysical systems: that of explaining evil as something negative. For evil is precisely that which is positive, that which makes itself palpable; and good on the other hand, i.e. all happiness and all gratification, is that which is negative, the mere abolition of a desire and extinction of a pain.

The most effective consolation in every misfortune and every affliction is to observe others who are more unfortunate than we: and everyone can do this. But what does that say for the condition of the whole?[2]

Schopenhauer's pessimism is often explained by pointing out how unhappy his childhood was given that his father was a moody and unhappy man, and that his mother a selfish and distant woman. No doubt there is some truth to this bit of psycho-diagnostics, it not just psychobabble. Yet, it is not all that important philosophically speaking. One could reach these same pessimistic conclusions simply on the basis of Schopenhauer's metaphysics, specifically and primarily on the basis of his concept of the underlying nature of reality, i.e., the will as manifested as insatiable striving. Schopenhauer makes this inference himself:

This great intensity of willing is in and by itself and directly a constant source of suffering, firstly because all willing as such springs from want, and hence suffering...Secondly because,

73

through the causal connection of things, most desires must remain unfulfilled, and the will is much more often crossed than satisfied. Consequently, much intense willing always entails much intense suffering. For all suffering is nothing but unfulfilled and thwarted willing...[3]

If willing, as it is understood by Schopenhauer, is insatiable striving, then by our very nature, or to put it differently and more strongly, as a matter of logic, it is impossible for us to be satisfied. And, if unsatisfied willing is painful, then we are doomed to a painful existence. It is unavoidable. It doesn't matter if one is emphatically and happily optimistic, or cheerlessly pessimistic, the message is a depressing negative one. The honestly optimistic are, if we believe Schopenhauer's account of the world, simply deluding themselves. They somehow, via temperament, stupidity, or self-deception, manage to convince themselves, and by their examples, others as well, that there is hope. One can quarrel with the metaphysics that lies behind Schopenhauer's pessimism, but not with its implications.

Schopenhauer is sometimes accused of being a *nihilist*, which is someone who holds that life has no value, that nothing we do, or can do, makes any difference whatever. The author of Ecclesiastes, possibly Solomon, expresses nihilism when he claims, "all is vanity, and vexation of the spirit." In contemporary philosophy, it is represented in the work of Albert Camus and Thomas Nagel. Nagel argues that we cannot help taking ourselves seriously, but that nothing we undertake, nor could undertake, can be justified.[4] Nothing can be justified, according to Nagel, because our whole system of justification is itself flawed. Justifications come to an end, and they do so because in order for us to justify anything we have to accept justifications that are not final justifications, because there are no final justifications. This is nihilism based upon skepticism. Camus is also a nihilist of basically the same sort as Nagel. But his way of coping with nihilism is different from Nagel. Camus claims that the realization that life is without value is just cause for the contemplation of suicide, which in turn serves as a springboard out of his dilemma. He can now turn his back on suicide, thrust his clenched fist towards the sky, and defy the fates. For Camus, this dramatic gesture constitutes "courageous defiance." About which one can only, somewhat smugly, ask, "Does this mean that you value courageous defiance?" If he answers our question with what we know he wants to say, namely, yes, then he contradicts his basic idea that nothing has any value. But if he says no,

74

then it seems to follow that any response to the fates would be *equally* appropriate. Why not cry, whine, and blubber in a most unmanly way? Nagel regards Camus' way of coping as "romantic" and "slightly self-pitying." He refuses to recognize any need for coping. As he views the matter, the problem concerning the meaning of our lives is a result of our ability to "transcend ourselves in thought," and this ability is one of our "most advanced and interesting characteristics." We should, he advises, "approach our absurd lives with irony instead of heroism or despair."[5]

Schopenhauer does not have to face this kind of problem. Instead of maintaining, as the nihilist does, that life has no meaning because nothing matters, he claims that it does have a meaning, and that its meaning is negative. Suicide for Schopenhauer is not a springboard for leaping into some form of romanticism. For him, unlike Kant, it is neither morally wrong nor should it be legally prohibited. However, even though suicide seems to provide a release from the torments of existence, Schopenhauer does not recommend it. It actually accomplishes nothing. Since the will is the same in all of us, and since it is in-itself indestructible, nothing is really gained by suicide. Escape from ceaseless striving is not possible! His idea that we are all ultimately one (will) and are in this sense indestructible is Schopenhauer's non-mythical formulation of the Indian, Asian, and Platonic idea of transmigration of souls.

Twentieth century nihilists often describe human existence as absurd. Both Camus and Nagel are fond of this way of putting their point. Nagel refines this claim by applying analytical techniques to the topic. He first provides an analysis of the way we ordinarily use the word 'absurd.' We use it, according to his analysis, to describe instances like the one of someone's trousers falling down around his ankles just as he is about to be knighted. According to Nagel, the reason we describe such an event as absurd is because there is a discrepancy between aspiration and reality. The subject aspires to the fulfillment of his wildest dream, but suffers humiliation instead. Having established by this example and others as well the essential meaning of 'absurd,' Nagel then asks what it would mean to say of *all* human existence that it is absurd. His answer is that each and every act by each and every human would have to involve a discrepancy between aspiration and reality. He then argues that this condition is met because of the discrepancy that always obtains between our taking our actions seriously and our inability to justify them. Although Schopenhauer is not a nihilist, one could, taking a lead from Nagel, argue that his pessimism also entails that human existence is absurd.

According to Schopenhauer, we are nothing more than manifestations of the will, or in other words, we are ultimately insatiable striving. We cannot help but strive to accomplish various goals, but their accomplishment cannot satisfy. What could be more absurd than this? There is of necessity always a discrepancy between our efforts to satisfy our needs and our ability to do so. Viewed in this fashion, it certainly seems that the upshot of both nihilism and pessimism is the same! Does Schopenhauer offer *any* hope? I will attempt to answer this question in the final section of this chapter when I consider what Schopenhauer has to say about the role of asceticism. Before I do so, however, I will turn to his views regarding morality.

Ethics is that part of philosophy that concerns itself with obligation, with what we "ought" to do. There are at least four basic approaches to ethics: ethical egoism, virtue ethics, consequentialism, and duty ethics. Psychological egoism is not an ethical theory, but it often plays an important role for the ethical egoist. Psychological egoists argue that all of us always act in our own self-interest. Ethical egoists, who accept psychological egoism, and most do, argue that since it is impossible to act for the sake of others, the only realistic approach to ethics is to argue that one *ought* always to act in ones own self-interest. Hobbes was an ethical egoist. Virtue ethicists, following Aristotle, argue that obligation must be defined in terms of virtues. The good or ethical person is a virtuous person. Doing the right thing for the virtue ethicists is doing what a good or virtuous person does. Virtue ethicists differ among themselves regarding what they accept as virtues. Consequentialists, primarily the utilitarians led by Bentham and Mill, maintain that obligation must be defined in terms of consequences. A good or ethically correct action is one that has the best consequences. Duty ethicists, Kant is the paradigm, argue that the *a priori* moral law, an abstraction, dictates, through reason, our moral obligations. Morality is categorical. There are no exceptions. The test of moral fortitude is the possession of right willedness. According to Kant, we must refrain from doing anything that we cannot will to be a universal law for all mankind. This precept is referred to as the "categorical imperative."

Although Schopenhauer strongly rejects Kant's approach to ethics, he incorporates elements from all three of the other approaches. Schopenhauer is not, however, primarily an ethicist. He is not concerned with regulating how we ought to conduct our lives. He is primarily interested in understanding the basis of morality, a fact reflected in the title of his essay *On The Basis of Morality*.

The single most important explanation for the existence of morality—its basis—is, according to Schopenhauer, our capacity for compassion. Without it, ethics would be, according to him, impossible. In a world the fundamental reality of which is blind, ceaseless striving, or will, morality is an enigma, explicable only because we are able to transcend our basic nature, our own selfish striving, and view others compassionately or with "loving kindness." Humans are essentially egoistic. They are also, fortunately, compassionate, and, unfortunately, malicious. We are all basically egoistic, so in order for us to live together harmoniously, we must learn to corral our basic impulses.[6] This idea Schopenhauer shares with Hobbes, and he credits Hobbes accordingly. The state, Schopenhauer tells us, "is set up on the correct assumption that pure morality is not to be expected." It is set up to protect us from "the injurious consequences of egoism arising out of the plurality of egoistic individuals."[7] We are social beings from necessity. Our own interests are paramount, and the egoistic interests of another which are not interlaced with our own interests would be of no interest to us at all were it not for the fact that we are capable of compassion. As I see it, what Schopenhauer is saying is that because our inner selves are all instantiations or phenomenal representations of the *same* underlying will, in knowing ourselves, we know all other human beings. Through self-awareness and self-knowledge we are able to "peer" into another person's mind and grasp that other person's needs, desires, etc. But because we know what it is like to be disappointed, we are able to transfer our own pain upon another, and as a result, we feel the other person's pain. This is compassion. Without it, we would be a race of unfeeling creatures, whose only notion of morality would have to be based upon a Kantian sense of duty, which for Schopenhauer is empty and unrealistic.[8] Compassion for Schopenhauer is responsible for the virtues of natural justice and benevolence, and for him these are the only virtues, a view with which one of the more important ethicists of the last sixty years, William Frankena, concurs. Frankena claims that:

> It seems to me that all the usual virtues (such as love, courage, temperance, honesty, gratitude, and considerateness), at least insofar as they are *moral* virtues, can be derived from these two. Insofar as a disposition cannot be derived from benevolence and justice, I should try to argue either that it is not a *moral* virtue (e.g., I take faith, hope, and wisdom to be religious or intellectual,

not moral virtues) or that it is not a virtue at all.[9]

Malice, the dark side of human nature, works against compassion, according to Schopenhauer. We often use our insights into the motives, desires, and needs of other humans and animals as a means for frustrating and causing them pain simply for our own amusement. Compassion and malice are both, for Schopenhauer, impulses that are antithetical to egoism. Compassion leads us to act antithetical to our own interests by aiding others. Malice compels us, on occasion, to do unto others what can undo us. If other humans recognize that we are prone to actions that are malicious, that fact causes them to distrust us, to disapprove of us, to avoid us, all of which is hurtful to us. These competing impulses, compassion and malice, are the foundations on which, according to Schopenhauer, moral praise and blame are based. We praise compassionate individuals and we blame the malicious ones. But there is something suspicious about this account of the matter. It seems to overlook the fact that we also condemn individuals for being selfish and egoistic. Schopenhauer recognizes this fact and tries to explain it away by arguing that we sometimes confuse fear with moral blame.

Schopenhauer's metaphysics of the will makes blaming one for being highly self-motivated as pointless as blaming someone for being red-haired. Self-concern or egoism is just a manifestation of what cannot be otherwise. It is in the nature of things. We fear other humans when we suspect that their desires are in conflict with our own, and blaming them for being selfish is our way of enlisting other members of society on our behalf. But, this form of moral blame is empty, and misplaced. Only pure malice is, according to Schopenhauer, subject to moral disapprobation. The reader may feel unconvinced, however, and want further evidence of this alleged fact. Richard Taylor in his essay on Schopenhauer's morality argues in favor of Schopenhauer's view as follows:

> What men do morally condemn is pure malice, and this is the only thing that unfailingly stamps an act and its agent with the deepest moral opprobrium. That a man should trample on others from the selfish egoism of his nature is not incomprehensible. It is a natural and inevitable part of social life. But that a man should, from no egoistic impulse at all, and even at considerable trouble and expense to himself, make the suffering of another the very object of his will—this, and this alone, morally outrages.[10]

78

I suspect that Taylor's answer is the appropriate one for Schopenhauer, but I do not agree that it is true. While some theologians regard pure malice as the essence of the Satan, I simply do not see how anyone could consider *most* purely malicious acts to be as morally objectionable as what the Nazis did to the Jews. Clearly, they were motivated by egoistic, and not purely malicious impulses. Equally clearly, what they did is paradigmatically of the *deepest* moral reprehensibility!

At any rate, in spite of the fact that even though Schopenhauer was more interested in explaining the basis for morality than in generating a normative or workable ethic, it would not be too hard to construct on the basis of what we have learned, an interesting and viable ethical approach, which I will designate, *integrated eclecticism*. As we have seen, he does offer a justification of a contract ethics of the sort devised by Hobbes, an ethics that I regard to be a formulation and enactment of folk ethics, an ethics that makes it possible for us to live together harmoniously. It is to that extent consequentialistic. His ethics also integrates a virtue ethics of sorts, but one that includes only two virtues, both of which are founded upon compassion. It provides us with a model for how we ought to act, as must any virtue ethics. The model it promotes is that of the saintly person consumed with her love for others, and her desire to do what she can to end human misery, a Mother Teresa. It is essentially egoistic, and thus adopts that aspect of egoistic ethics that forgives the relentless pursuit of one's own interests.

I want now to turn to Schopenhauer's views regarding asceticism. It is with asceticism that he finds cause for hope. In book four of *The World as Will and Representation*, in one of its most powerful passages, after he reminds us that contemplation of the beautiful can momentarily transport us above all willing, above all our desires and cares, and rid us of ourselves, he says:

> And we know that these moments, when, delivered from the fierce pressure of the will, we emerge, as it were, from the heavy atmosphere of the earth, are the most blissful that we experience. From this we can infer how blessed must be the life of a man whose will is silenced, not for a few moments, as in the enjoyment of the beautiful, but for ever, indeed completely extinguished, except for the last glimmering spark that maintains the body and is extinguished with it. Such a man...is then left

79

only as pure knowing being, as the undimmed mirror of the world. Nothing can distress or alarm him any more; nothing can any longer move him; for he has cut all the thousand threads of willing which hold us bound to the world, and which as craving, fear, envy, and anger drag us here and there in constant pain.[11]

We must not get too hopeful, however, for, as he notes a few paragraphs further on, "we must not imagine that, after the denial of the will-to-live has once appeared through knowledge that has become a quieter of the will, such denial no longer wavers or falters." Quite the contrary, "it must always be achieved afresh by constant struggle...on earth no one can have lasting peace."[12] The ascetic must struggle everyday to find release from the will. It is in this context that such courses of action as the "Noble Eightfold Path" of the Buddha, which I laid out on page 5 above, becomes relevant. Schopenhauer stresses the unpleasant side of asceticism, however, according to him, the ascetic should seek to break the hold that will has on him by seeking out the disagreeable, "the voluntarily chosen way of life of penance and self-chastisement, for the constant mortification of the will." In fact he "defines" asceticism this way.

There are, however, others ways to conceive of asceticism. It has a long tradition both in the East and in the West. Epicurus and his followers were ascetics of a very different sort from those Schopenhauer had in mind when he offered his definition of the expression 'asceticism.' They avoided the unpleasant and disagreeable. But they made every effort to conquer their passions. Their goal was to reach a state of contentment, free from the strivings for success, fame, wealth, and glory. Contentment for them was freedom from pain. They strove to maximize this state of being. Striving for them, as for Schopenhauer, was of two sorts. On the one hand there is seeking success, fame, glory, and wealth, which, more often than not, leads to disappointment and pain. But pursuing a path of restraint, the second form of striving, was, for the Epicureans, not only acceptable, it was laudable. Whereas, for Schopenhauer, the acceptable or praiseworthy path was facing the disagreeable—enduring pain for the sake of freedom. For both Epicurus and Schopenhauer the strivings of everyday life were something to be conquered, but Epicurus, unlike Schopenhauer, was not pessimistic. He was basically optimistic.

Although it is not altogether clear who is right on this issue, there is certainly at least as much evidence in favor of the Epicurean form of asceticism as there is for Schopenhauer's. One observation that favors the Epicurean perspective is that our ordinary concept of 'being satiated" is often said to be true of an individual who has reached her/his goal. According to this conception, it is false that every realization of a goal terminates in a state of being unsatisfied. An addict *is* someone who exemplifies the kind of insatiability that Schopenhauer attributes to will, so do compulsive personalities. In youth, one is often unsure what one wants to do. This causes one to be restless and distressed. The teens and twenties are often painful. But most of us are not addicts or compulsive personalities, and, fortunately, most of us pass through our youth without suffering permanent damage. What is important to realize is that addicts, compulsives, teenagers, and malcontents, are the exception rather than the rule.

Life is indeed difficult. There is an immense amount of pain and suffering in the world. We reside in an environment in which any number of calamities can occur at any time. Hurricanes, earthquakes, tornados, deadly bacteria, incurable viruses, terminal deceases, etc., impinge upon us with great frequency. If we dwell on the possibility of these calamities, and add to this thought the incredibly cruel and monstrous things that other humans are capable of doing to any of us, a very sobering state of mind is the likely result. Through an ethics of the contract and consequentialistic variety, what I prefer to call, as I indicated previously, "folk ethics," we are able to control to a large extent the horrors that other humans perpetrate upon us. But, as yet, we can do very little about natural disasters. Science is our only hope for the minimization of these catastrophes. It has already done a lot to minimize them. But can it offer any hope for those who like Schopenhauer are convinced that the universe is fundamentally insatiable striving? Of course not! For many of us, however, his way of viewing the matter remains an alien viewpoint. Fortunately, it is possible to view the underlying energy or life force that Schopenhauer considers to be the will quite differently from the way he views it.

Why not view the fact that we do not, upon the accomplishment of one of our goals, find ultimate satisfaction or complete satiation as an asset rather than a flaw? There is, in fact, something rather pathetic about Schopenhauer's craving for satiation. His recommendation that we adopt asceticism and use it to escape from this world of kinetic, never ending energy is somehow to get it backwards. What keeps us from being bored, what keeps us feeling alive, what provides most of us our very reason for living, *is* the fact that there is no final goal, no end to the ongoing energy that is our essence. Trying to escape from what is *for us* just possibly somewhere near the next best thing to the best of all possible worlds makes very little sense. Better to improve upon it and find the means to lengthen our stay in it. At the very least this perspective is no less persuasive or valid than Schopenhauer's.

For those who require or seek it, there is also another means for coping with the uncertainty and unfulfilling nature of human existence. That means is mysticism. Asceticism and mysticism are two different, though often related, phenomena. What is often referred to as a mystical state is sometimes referred to as a transcendent state, and even as ecstasy. For Schopenhauer, the mystical state is a transitory phenomenon. It provides an inducement for the ascetic to continue to pursue the disagreeable. For him it is intertwined with asceticism, and is understood, as is the aesthetic experience, as a "quieter" of the will. There is no cogent reason for buying this conception, however. I have in fact argued elsewhere that mystical experiences are self-justifying experiences; that they are ends in themselves; that they are of intrinsic worth; that the person experiencing them recognizes them as such; that such experiences can and do occur in non-ascetic and non-religious and non-aesthetic contexts; and finally that they can occur quite by chance, and are not always the result of an intentional effort to produce them.[13]

Mystical experiences, which William James describes as "illuminations, revelations, full of significance and importance," and about which "one feels no adequate report of its [their] contents can be given in words" are referred to in Indian philosophy and religion as *Nirvana*. They manifest themselves in a variety of differing kinds of circumstance. Such an experience can result during any kind of daring or dangerous activity, in warfare, during an automobile accident, while skydiving, or foxhunting, or bull fighting. Whenever it occurs, either as a result of ascetic effort, in the presence of great art, by daring, or by chance as in an accident, etc., it is its own reward, and no one who has such an experience is ever quite the same afterwards. To the extent that one has had such experiences, one's life can be said to be non-absurd and meaningful. And for those who have had such an experience, it cancels out pessimism or any other essentially negative view of life.

None of the difficulties I have posed for, nor the alternatives I juxtaposed to, Schopenhauer's perspective are meant to diminish his importance. The stimulation his views initiate is sufficient in itself to guarantee his lasting worth. Take a painting by Cézanne, juxtapose it to one by Rembrandt, I prefer the Rembrandt. I have friends who prefer Cézanne. But we all agree that they are both great artists, and that we are extremely fortunate to have their differing visions of the world. It is possible to find fault with certain aspects of each, but that does not take away from their greatness. Without the work of Cézanne, Rembrandt, or Schopenhauer, the world would be greatly diminished.

---

[1] Schopenhauer (1969) Vol. I, p. 322.
[2] Schopenhauer (1980) pp. 25-26.
[3] Schopenhauer (1969) Vol. I, p. 363.
[4] For an exposition and critique of Nagel, see Odell (1983-C).
[5] Nagel (1981) p. 161.
[6] Schopenhauer (1965) pp. 130-147.
[7] Schopenhauer (1969) Vol. I, p. 345.
[8] Schopenhauer (1965) pp. 49-119.
[9] Frankena (1973) p. 65.
[10] Taylor (1980) p. 104.
[11] Schopenhauer (1969) Vol. I, p. 390.
[12] Ibid., p. 391.
[13] Odell (1983-C) pp. 244-248.

Selected Bibliography

Austin, J. L. (1962) *Sense and Sensibilia* (Oxford: The Clarendon Press).

Bambrough, J. R. (1960) "Universals and Family Resemblances," *PAS*, LXI.

Campbell, Keith (1990) *Abstract Particulars* (Oxford: Basil Blackwell ltd.).

Fox, Michael (1980) *Schopenhauer: His Philosophical Achievement* (Oxford: Oxford University Press).

Frankena, William (1973) *Ethics*, 2nd edition (Englewood Cliffs, New Jersey: Prentice-Hall Inc.).

Hacker, P. M. S. (1996) *Wittgenstein's Place in Twentieth Century Philosophy* (Oxford: Blackwells).

Hamlyn, D. W. (1980) *Schopenhauer* (London: Routledge & Kegan Paul).

Höffding, Harold (1955) *A History of Modern Philosophy* (United States: Dover Publications, Inc.).

Kant, I. (1961) *Critique of Pure Reason* (London: MacMillan & Co LTD).

Klemke, E. D. (1981) *The Meaning of Life* (New York and Oxford: Oxford University Press).

Magee, Bryan (1983) *The Philosophy of Schopenhauer* (Oxford: Oxford University Press).

Nagel, Thomas (1981) "The Absurd" reprinted in, *The Meaning of Life*, ed. E. D. Klemke (Oxford: Oxford University Press).

Odell, S. Jack (1983-A) "Review of *Schopenhauer: His Philosophical Achievement*," Edited by Michael Fox, *Teaching Philosophy*, January, 1983.

Odell, S. Jack (1983-B) "Review of *Schopenhauer,*" by D. W. Hamlyn, *Teaching Philosophy* January, 1983.

(1983-C) "Life is Not Absurd," *Metaphilosophy*, Vol. 14, No. 3/4.

(1984) "A Paraphrastic Theory of Meaning," *Theoretical Linguistics*, Vol. 11, No. 3.

(1985) "Review of *The Philosophy of Schopenhauer*" by Brian Magee, *Teaching Philosophy*, July, 1985.

(2001) *On Moore* (Belmont California: Wadsworth).

Odell, S. Jack, and James Zartman, (1982) "A Defensible Formulation of the Verification Principle," *Metaphilosophy*, Vol. 13, No. 1, January 1982.

Plato (1963) *The Collected Dialogues of Plato*, 2nd printing, ed. Edith Hamilton and Huntington Cairns (New York: Pantheon Books).

Russell, Bertrand (1945) *The History of Western Philosophy: Its connection with Political and Social circumstances from the Earliest Times to the Present Day* (New York: Simon and Schuster).

Schopenhauer, A. (1980) "On the Suffering of the World," reprinted under this title in, *The Meaning of Life*, ed. S. Sanders and D. R. Cheney (Englewood Cliffs New Jersey: Prentice-Hall Inc.) pp. 25-32.

(1974) *The Fourfold Root of The Principle of Sufficient Reason*, translated by E. F. J. Payne (La Salle, Illinois: Open Court Publishing Company).

(1969) *The World as Will and Representation*, translated by E. F. J. Payne (New York: Dove Publications, Inc.).

(1965) *On the Basis of Morality*, translated by E. F. J. Payne (New York: Bobbs-Merrill).

Stroll, Avrum (1994) *Moore and Wittgenstein on Certainty* (Oxford: Oxford University Press).

Taylor, Richard (1980) "On the Basis of Morality," in Fox (1980).

Wittgenstein, L. (1958) *Philosophical Investigations* (Englewood Cliffs, New Jersey: Prentice Hall).

(1972) *On Certainty* (New York: Harper & Row).